Post-Synodal
Apostolic Exhortation
of His Holiness
Pope John Paul II

RECONCILIATION
AND PENANCE

In the Mission
of the Church Today

Reconciliatio et Paenitentia

auline
BOOKS & MEDIA

BOSTON

ISBN 0-8198-6430-7

Vatican translation

Printed and published in the U.S.A. by Pauline Books & Media, 50 Saint Pauls Avenue, Boston MA 02130-3491.

www.pauline.org

Pauline Books & Media is the publishing house of the Daughters of St. Paul, an international congregation of women religious serving the Church with the communications media.

5 6 7 8 9 10 11 12   09 08 07 06 05 04 03

Contents

Origin and Meaning
of the Document 7

A Shattered World 8

Longing for Reconciliation 10

The Synod's View... 10

Chapter I
Conversion and Reconciliation:
The Church's Task and Commitment 17
1. A Parable of Reconciliation...17

From the Brother Who Was Lost... 17

To the Brother Who Stayed at Home 18

2. At the Sources of Reconciliation 19

In the Light of Christ the Reconciler 19

The Reconciling Church 21

The Reconciled Church 23

3. God's Initiative and the Church's Ministry......................25

Reconciliation Comes from God 25

The Church, the Great Sacrament of Reconciliation 27

Other Means of Reconciliation 27

Chapter II

The Love That Is Greater Than Sin 31

The Tragedy of Man 31

1. The Mystery of Sin 33

Disobedience to God 33

Division Between Brothers 34

Personal Sin and Social Sin 35

Mortal and Venial 39

The Loss of the Sense of Sin 45

2. "Mysterium Pietatis" 49

It Is Christ Himself 50

The Effort of the Christian 52

Toward a Reconciled Life 52

Chapter III

The Pastoral Ministry of Penance
and Reconciliation 55

Promoting Penance and Reconciliation 55

1. The Promotion of Penance and Reconciliation:
Ways and Means 57

Dialogue 58

Catechesis 62

The Sacraments 68

2. The Sacrament of Penance
and Reconciliation 71

"Whose Sins You Shall Forgive" 72

The Sacrament of Forgiveness 76

Some Fundamental Convictions 77

Forms of Celebration 85

Celebration of the Sacrament with General Absolution 88

Some More Delicate Cases 90

Concluding Expression of Hope 91

Notes 95

Origin and Meaning
of the Document

1. To speak of reconciliation and penance is for the men and women of our time an invitation to rediscover, translated into their own way of speaking, the very words with which our savior and teacher Jesus Christ began his preaching: "Repent, and believe in the Gospel,"[1] that is to say, accept the good news of love, of adoption as children of God and hence of brotherhood.

Why does the church put forward once more this subject and this invitation?

The concern to know better and to understand modern man and the contemporary world, to solve their puzzle and reveal their mystery, to discern the ferments of good and evil within them, has long caused many people to direct at man and the world a questioning gaze. It is the gaze of the historian and sociologist, philosopher and theologian, psychologist and humanist, poet and mystic: Above all, it is the gaze, anxious yet full of hope, of the pastor.

In an exemplary fashion this is shown on every page of the important pastoral constitution of the Second Vatican Council *Gaudium et Spes* on the church in the modern world, particularly in its wide-ranging and penetrating introduction. It is likewise shown in certain documents issued through the wisdom and charity of my esteemed predecessors, whose admirable pontificates were marked by the historic and prophetic event of that ecumenical council.

In common with others, the pastor too can discern among the various unfortunate characteristics of the world and of humanity in our time the existence of many deep and painful divisions.

A Shattered World

2. These divisions are seen in the relationships between individuals and groups, and also at the level of larger groups: nations against nations and blocs of opposing countries in a headlong quest for domination. At the root of this alienation it is not hard to discern conflicts which, instead of being resolved through dialogue, grow more acute in confrontation and opposition.

Careful observers, studying the elements that cause division, discover reasons of the most widely differing kinds: from the growing disproportion between groups, social classes and countries, to ideological rivalries that are far from dead; from the opposition between economic interests to political polarization; from tribal differences to discrimination for social and religious reasons. Moreover, certain facts that are obvious to all constitute as it were the pitiful face of the division of which they are the fruit and demonstrate its seriousness in an inescapably concrete way. Among the many other painful social phenomena of our times one can note:

—The trampling upon the basic rights of the human person, the first of these being the right to life and to a worthy quality of life, which is all the more scandalous in that it coexists with a rhetoric never before known on these same rights.

—Hidden attacks and pressures against the freedom of individuals and groups, not excluding the freedom which is most offended against and threatened: the freedom to have, profess and practice one's own faith.

—The various forms of discrimination: racial, cultural, religious, etc.

—Violence and terrorism.

—The use of torture and unjust and unlawful methods of repression.

—The stockpiling of conventional or atomic weapons, the arms race with the spending on military purposes of sums which could be used to alleviate the undeserved misery of peoples that are socially and economically depressed.

—An unfair distribution of the world's resources and of the assets of civilization, which reaches its highest point in a type of social organization whereby the distance between the human conditions of the rich and the poor becomes ever greater.[2] The overwhelming power of this division makes the world in which we live a world shattered[3] to its very foundations.

Moreover, the church—without identifying herself with the world or being of the world—is in the world and is engaged in dialogue with the world.[4] It is therefore not surprising if one notices in the structure of the church herself repercussions and signs of the division affecting human society. Over and above the divisions between the Christian communions that have afflicted her for centuries, the church today is experiencing within herself sporadic divisions among her own members, divisions caused by differing views or options in the doctrinal and pastoral field.[5] These divisions too can at times seem incurable.

However disturbing these divisions may seem at first sight, it is only by a careful examination that one can detect their root: It is to be found in a wound in man's inmost self. In the light of faith we call it sin: beginning with original sin, which all of us bear from birth as an inheritance from our first parents, to the sin which each one of us commits when we abuse our own freedom.

Longing for Reconciliation

3. Nevertheless, that same inquiring gaze, if it is discerning enough, detects in the very midst of division an unmistakable desire among people of good will and true Christians to mend the divisions, to heal the wounds and to re-establish at all levels an essential unity. This desire arouses in many people a real longing for reconciliation even in cases where there is no actual use of this word.

Some consider reconciliation as an impossible dream which ideally might become the lever for a true transformation of society. For others it is to be gained by arduous efforts and therefore a goal to be reached through serious reflection and action. Whatever the case, the longing for sincere and consistent reconciliation is without a shadow of doubt a fundamental driving force in our society, reflecting an irrepressible desire for peace. And it is as strongly so as the factors of division, even though this is a paradox.

But reconciliation cannot be less profound than the division itself. The longing for reconciliation and reconciliation itself will be complete and effective only to the extent that they reach—in order to heal it—that original wound which is the root of all other wounds: namely sin.

The Synod's View

4. Therefore every institution or organization concerned with serving people and saving them in their fundamental dimensions must closely study reconciliation in order to grasp more fully its meaning and significance and in order to draw the necessary practical conclusions.

The church of Jesus Christ could not fail to make this study. With the devotion of a mother and the understanding of a teacher, she earnestly and carefully applies herself to detecting in society not only the signs of division but also the no less

10

eloquent and significant signs of the quest for reconciliation. For she knows that she especially has been given the ability and assigned the mission to make known the true and profoundly religious meaning of reconciliation and its full scope. She is thereby already helping to clarify the essential terms of the question of unity and peace.

My predecessors constantly preached reconciliation and invited to reconciliation the whole of humanity and every section and portion of the human community that they saw wounded and divided.[6] And I myself, by an interior impulse which—I am certain—was obeying both an inspiration from on high and the appeals of humanity, decided to emphasize the subject of reconciliation and to do this in two ways, each of them solemn and exacting. In the first place, by convoking the Sixth General Assembly of the Synod of Bishops; in the second place, by making reconciliation the center of the jubilee year called to celebrate the 1,950th anniversary of the redemption.[7] Having to assign a theme to the synod, I found myself fully in accord with the one suggested by many of my brothers in the episcopate, namely, the fruitful theme of reconciliation in close connection with the theme of penance.[8]

The term and the very concept of penance are very complex. If we link penance with the *metanoia* which the synoptics refer to, it means the inmost change of heart under the influence of the word of God and in the perspective of the kingdom.[9] But penance also means changing one's life in harmony with the change of heart, and in this sense doing penance is completed by bringing forth fruits worthy of penance:[10] It is one's whole existence that becomes penitential, that is to say, directed toward a continuous striving for what is better. But doing penance is something authentic and effective only if it is translated into deeds and acts of penance. In this sense penance means, in the Christian theological and spiritual vocabulary, asceticism, that is to say, the concrete daily effort of a person, supported by God's

11

grace, to lose his or her own life for Christ as the only means of gaining it;[11] an effort to put off the old man and put on the new;[12] an effort to overcome in oneself what is of the flesh in order that what is spiritual[13] may prevail; a continual effort to rise from the things of here below to the things of above, where Christ is.[14] Penance is therefore a conversion that passes from the heart to deeds and then to the Christian's whole life.

In each of these meanings penance is closely connected with reconciliation, for reconciliation with God, with oneself and with others implies overcoming that radical break which is sin. And this is achieved only through the interior transformation or conversion which bears fruit in a person's life through acts of penance.

The basic document of the synod (also called the *lineamenta*), which was prepared with the sole purpose of presenting the theme while stressing certain fundamental aspects of it, enabled the ecclesial communities throughout the world to reflect for almost two years on these aspects of a question—that of conversion and reconciliation—which concerns everyone. It also enabled them to draw from it a fresh impulse for the Christian life and apostolate. That reflection was further deepened in the more immediate preparation for the work of the synod, thanks to the *instrumentum laboris* which was sent in due course to the bishops and their collaborators. After that, the synod fathers, assisted by all those called to attend the actual sessions, spent a whole month assiduously dealing with the theme itself and with the numerous and varied questions connected with it. There emerged from the discussions, from the common study and from the diligent and accurate work done, a large and precious treasure which the final *propositiones* sum up in their essence.

The synod's view does not ignore the acts of reconciliation (some of which pass almost unobserved in their daily ordinariness) which, though in differing degrees, serve to resolve the many tensions, to overcome the many conflicts and to conquer the divisions both large and small by restoring unity. But the synod's main concern was to discover in the depth of these scattered acts the hidden root—reconciliation so to speak "at the source," which takes place in people's hearts and minds.

The church's charism and likewise her unique nature vis-a-vis reconciliation, at whatever level it needs to be achieved, lie in the fact that she always goes back to that reconciliation at the source. For by reason of her essential mission, the church feels an obligation to go to the roots of that original wound of sin in order to bring healing and to re-establish, so to speak, an equally original reconciliation which will be the effective principle of all true reconciliation. This is the reconciliation which the church had in mind and which she put forward through the synod.

Sacred Scripture speaks to us of this reconciliation, inviting us to make every effort to attain it.[15] But Scripture also tells us that it is above all a merciful gift of God to humanity.[16] The history of salvation—the salvation of the whole of humanity as well as of every human being of whatever period—is the wonderful history of a reconciliation: the reconciliation whereby God, as Father, in the blood and the cross of his Son made man, reconciles the world to himself and thus brings into being a new family of those who have been reconciled.

Reconciliation becomes necessary because there has been the break of sin from which derive all the other forms of break within man and about him. Reconciliation, therefore, in order to be complete necessarily requires liberation from sin, which is to be rejected in its deepest roots. Thus a close internal link unites conversion and reconciliation. It is impossible to split these two realities or to speak of one and say nothing of the other.

The synod at the same time spoke about the reconciliation of the whole human family and of the conversion of the heart of every individual, of his or her return to God: It did so because it wished to recognize and proclaim the fact that there can be no union among people without an internal change in each individual. Personal conversion is the necessary path to harmony between individuals.[17] When the church proclaims the good news of reconciliation or proposes achieving it through the sacraments, she is exercising a truly prophetic role, condemning the evils of man in their infected source, showing the root of divisions and bringing hope in the possibility of overcoming tensions and conflict and reaching brotherhood, concord and peace at all levels and in all sections of human society. She is changing a historical condition of hatred and violence into a civilization of love. She is offering to everyone the evangelical and sacramental principle of that reconciliation at the source, from which comes every other gesture or act of reconciliation, also at the social level.

It is this reconciliation, the result of conversion, which is dealt with in the present apostolic exhortation. For, as happened at the end of the three previous assemblies of the synod, this time too the fathers who had taken part presented the conclusions of the synod's work to the bishop of Rome, the universal pastor of the church and the head of the College of Bishops, in his capacity as president of the synod. I accepted as a serious and welcome duty of my ministry the task of drawing from the enormous abundance of the synod in order to offer to the people of God, as the fruit of the same synod, a doctrinal and pastoral message on the subject of penance and reconciliation. In the first part I shall speak of the church in the carrying out of her mission of reconciliation, in the work of the conversion of hearts in order to bring about a renewed embrace between man and God, man and his brother, man and the whole of creation. In the second part there will be indicated the radical cause of all wounds and divisions between people, and in the first place between people and God: namely sin. Afterward I shall indicate the means that enable the church to promote and encourage full reconciliation between people and God and, as a consequence, of people with one another.

The document which I now entrust to the sons and daughters of the church and also to all those who, whether they are believers or not, look to the church with interest and sincerity, is meant to be a fitting response to what the synod asked of me. But it is also—and I wish to say this clearly as a duty to truth and justice—something produced by the synod itself. For the contents of these pages come from the synod: from its remote and immediate preparation, from the *instrumentum laboris,* from the interventions in the Synod Hall and the *circuli minores,* and especially from the sixty-three *propositiones.* Here we have the result of the joint work of the fathers, who included the representatives of the Eastern churches, whose theological, spiritual and liturgical heritage is so rich and venerable, also with regard to the subject that concerns us here. Furthermore, it was the Council of the Synod Secretariat which evaluated, in two important sessions, the results and orientations of the synod assembly just after it had ended, which highlighted the dynamics of the already mentioned *propositiones* and which then indicated the lines considered most suitable for the preparation of the present document. I am grateful to all those who did this work and, in fidelity to my mission, I wish here to pass on the elements from the doctrinal and pastoral treasure of the synod which seem to me providential for people's lives at this magnificent yet difficult moment in history.

It is appropriate—and very significant—to do this while there remains fresh in people's minds the memory of the Holy Year, which was lived in the spirit of penance, conversion and reconciliation. May this exhortation, entrusted to my brothers in the episcopate and to their collaborators, the priests and deacons, to men and women religious, and to all men and women of upright conscience, be a means of purification, enrichment and deepening in personal faith. May it also be a leaven capable of encouraging the growth in the midst of the world of peace and brotherhood, hope and joy—values which spring from the

Gospel as it is accepted, meditated upon and lived day by day after the example of Mary, mother of our Lord Jesus Christ, through whom it pleased God to reconcile all things to himself.[18]

Chapter I

Conversion and Reconciliation: The Church's Task and Commitment

1. A Parable of Reconciliation

5. At the beginning of this apostolic exhortation there comes into my mind that extraordinary passage in St. Luke, the deeply religious as well as human substance of which I have already sought to illustrate in a previous document.[19] I refer to the parable of the prodigal son.[20]

From the Brother Who Was Lost...

"There was a man who had two sons; the younger of them said to his father, 'Father, give me the share of property that falls to me,' " says Jesus as he begins the dramatic story of that young man: the adventurous departure from his father's house, the squandering of all his property in a loose and empty life, the dark days of exile and hunger, but even more of lost dignity, humiliation and shame and then nostalgia for his own home, the courage to go back, the father's welcome. The father had certainly not forgotten his son, indeed he had kept unchanged his affection and esteem for him. So he had always waited for him, and now he embraces him and he gives orders for a great feast to celebrate the return of him who "was dead, and is alive; he was lost, and is found."

This prodigal son is man—every human being: bewitched

by the temptation to separate himself from his Father in order to lead his own independent existence; disappointed by the emptiness of the mirage which had fascinated him; alone, dishonored, exploited when he tries to build a world all for himself; sorely tried, even in the depths of his own misery, by the desire to return to communion with his Father. Like the father in the parable, God looks out for the return of his child, embraces him when he arrives and orders the banquet of the new meeting with which the reconciliation is celebrated.

The most striking element of the parable is the father's festive and loving welcome of the returning son: It is a sign of the mercy of God, who is always willing to forgive. Let us say at once: Reconciliation is principally a gift of the heavenly Father.

...To the Brother Who Stayed at Home

6. But the parable also brings into the picture the elder brother, who refuses to take his place at the banquet. He rebukes his younger brother for his dissolute wanderings, and he rebukes his father for the welcome given to the prodigal son while he himself, a temperate and hard-working person, faithful to father and home, has never been allowed—he says—to have a celebration with his friends. This is a sign that he does not understand the father's goodness. To the extent that this brother, too sure of himself and his own good qualities, jealous and haughty, full of bitterness and anger, is not converted and is not reconciled with his father and brother, the banquet is not yet fully the celebration of a reunion and rediscovery.

Man—every human being—is also this elder brother. Selfishness makes him jealous, hardens his heart, blinds him and shuts him off from other people and from God. The loving kindness and mercy of the father irritate and enrage him; for him the happiness of the brother who has been found again has a bitter taste.[21] From this point of view he too needs to be converted in order to be reconciled.

The parable of the prodigal son is above all the story of the inexpressible love of a Father—God—who offers to his son when he comes back to him the gift of full reconciliation. But when the parable evokes, in the figure of the elder son, the selfishness which divides the brothers, it also becomes the story of the human family: It describes our situation and shows the path to be followed. The prodigal son, in his anxiety for conversion, to return to the arms of his father and to be forgiven, represents those who are aware of the existence in their inmost hearts of a longing for reconciliation at all levels and without reserve, and who realize with an inner certainty that this reconciliation is possible only if it derives from a first and fundamental reconciliation—the one which brings a person back from distant separation to filial friendship with God, whose infinite mercy is clearly known. But if the parable is read from the point of view of the other son, it portrays the situation of the human family, divided by forms of selfishness. It throws light on the difficulty involved in satisfying the desire and longing for one reconciled and united family. It therefore reminds us of the need for a profound transformation of hearts through the rediscovery of the Father's mercy and through victory over misunderstanding and over hostility among brothers and sisters.

In the light of this inexhaustible parable of the mercy that wipes out sin, the church takes up the appeal that the parable contains and grasps her mission of working, in imitation of the Lord, for the conversion of hearts and for the reconciliation of people with God and with one another—these being two realities that are intimately connected.

2. At the Sources of Reconciliation
In the Light of Christ the Reconciler

7. As we deduce from the parable of the prodigal son, reconciliation is a gift of God, an initiative on his part. But our

faith teaches us that this initiative takes concrete form in the mystery of Christ the redeemer, the reconciler and the liberator of man from sin in all its forms. St. Paul likewise does not hesitate to sum up in this task and function the incomparable mission of Jesus of Nazareth, the word and the Son of God made man.

We too can start with this central mystery of the economy of salvation, the key to St. Paul's Christology. "If while we were enemies we were reconciled to God by the death of his Son," writes St. Paul, "much more, now that we are reconciled, shall we be saved by his life. Not only so, but we also rejoice in God through our Lord Jesus Christ, through whom we have now received our reconciliation."[22] Therefore, since "God was in Christ reconciling the world to himself," Paul feels inspired to exhort the Christians of Corinth: "Be reconciled to God."[23]

This mission of reconciliation through death on the cross is spoken of in another terminology by the evangelist John, when he observes that Christ had to die "to gather into one the children of God who are scattered abroad."[24]

But it is once more St. Paul who enables us to broaden our vision of Christ's work to cosmic dimensions when he writes that in Christ the Father has reconciled to himself all creatures, those in heaven and those on earth.[25] It can rightly be said of Christ the redeemer that "in the time of wrath he was taken in exchange"[26] and that, if he is "our peace,"[27] he is also our reconciliation.

With every good reason his passion and death, sacramentally renewed in the eucharist, are called by the liturgy the "sacrifice of reconciliation":[28] reconciliation with God and with the brethren, since Jesus teaches that fraternal reconciliation must take place before the sacrifice is offered.[29]

Beginning with these and other significant passages in the New Testament, we can therefore legitimately relate all our reflections on the whole mission of Christ to his mission as the one who reconciles. Thus there must be proclaimed once more the church's belief in Christ's redeeming act, in the paschal mystery of his death and resurrection, as the cause of man's reconciliation in its twofold aspect of liberation from sin and communion of grace with God.

It is precisely before the sad spectacle of the divisions and difficulties in the way of reconciliation between people that I invite all to look to the *mysterium crucis* as the loftiest drama in which Christ perceives and suffers to the greatest possible extent the tragedy of the division of man from God, so that he cries out in the words of the psalmist: "My God, my God, why have you forsaken me?"[30] and at the same time accomplishes our reconciliation. With our eyes fixed on the mystery of Golgotha we should be reminded always of that "vertical" dimension of division and reconciliation concerning the relationship between man and God, a dimension which in the eyes of faith always prevails over the "horizontal" dimension, that is to say, over the reality of division between people and the need for reconciliation between them. For we know that reconciliation between people is and can only be the fruit of the redemptive act of Christ, who died and rose again to conquer the kingdom of sin, to re-establish the covenant with God and thus break down the dividing wall[31] which sin had raised up between people.

The Reconciling Church

8. But, as Pope St. Leo said, speaking of Christ's passion, "Everything that the Son of God did and taught for the reconciliation of the world we know not only from the history of his past actions, but we experience it also in the effectiveness of what he accomplishes in the present."[32] We experience the reconciliation which he accomplished in his humanity in the efficacy of the sacred mysteries which are celebrated by his church, for which he gave his life and which he established as the sign and also the means of salvation.

This is stated by St. Paul when he writes that God has given to Christ's apostles a share in his work of reconciliation. He says: "God...gave us the ministry of reconciliation...and the message of reconciliation."[33]

To the hands and lips of the apostles, his messengers, the Father has mercifully entrusted a ministry of reconciliation, which they carry out in a singular way by virtue of the power to act *in persona Christi.* But the message of reconciliation has also been entrusted to the whole community of believers, to the whole fabric of the church, that is to say, the task of doing everything possible to witness to reconciliation and to bring it about in the world.

It can be said that the Second Vatican Council too, in defining the church as a "sacrament—a sign and instrument, that is, of communion with God and of unity among all people," and in indicating as the church's function that of obtaining "full unity in Christ" for the "people of the present day...drawn ever more closely together by social, technical and cultural bonds,"[34] recognized that the church must strive above all to bring all people to full reconciliation.

In intimate connection with Christ's mission, one can therefore sum up the church's mission, rich and complex as it is, as being her central task of reconciling people: with God, with themselves, with neighbor, with the whole of creation; and this in a permanent manner since, as I said on another occasion, "the church is also by her nature always reconciling."[35]

The church is reconciling inasmuch as she proclaims the message of reconciliation as she has always done throughout her history, from the apostolic Council of Jerusalem[36] down to the latest synod and the recent jubilee of the redemption. The originality of this proclamation is in the fact that for the church reconciliation is closely linked with conversion of heart: This is the necessary path to understanding among human beings.

The church is also reconciling inasmuch as she shows man

the paths and offers the means for reaching this fourfold reconciliation. The paths are precisely those of conversion of heart and victory over sin, whether this latter is selfishness or injustice, arrogance or exploitation of others, attachment to material goods or the unrestrained quest for pleasure. The means are those of faithful and loving attention to God's word; personal and community prayer; and in particular the sacraments, true signs and instruments of reconciliation, among which there excels, precisely under this aspect, the one which we are rightly accustomed to call the sacrament of reconciliation or penance and to which we shall return later on.

The Reconciled Church

9. My venerable predecessor Paul VI commendably highlighted the fact that the church, in order to evangelize, must begin by showing that she herself has been evangelized, that is to say, that she is open to the full and complete proclamation of the good news of Jesus Christ in order to listen to it and put it into practice.[37] I too, by bringing together in one document the reflections of the fourth general assembly of the synod, have spoken of a church that is catechized to the extent that she carries out catechesis.[38]

I now do not hesitate to resume the comparison, insofar as it applies to the theme I am dealing with, in order to assert that the church, if she is to be reconciling, must begin by being a reconciled church. Beneath this simple and indicative expression lies the conviction that the church, in order ever more effectively to proclaim and propose reconciliation to the world, must become ever more genuinely a community of disciples of Christ (even though it were only "the little flock" of the first days), united in the commitment to be continually converted to the Lord and to live as new people in the spirit and practice of reconciliation.

To the people of our time, so sensitive to the proof of concrete living witness, the church is called upon to give an example of reconciliation particularly within herself. And for this purpose we must all work to bring peace to people's minds, to reduce tensions, to overcome divisions and to heal wounds that may have been inflicted by brother on brother when the contrast of choices in the field of what is optional becomes acute; and on the contrary we must try to be united in what is essential for Christian faith and life, in accordance with the ancient maxim: In what is doubtful, freedom; in what is necessary, unity; in all things, charity.

It is in accordance with this same criterion that the church must conduct her ecumenical activity. For in order to be completely reconciled, she knows that she must continue the quest for unity among those who are proud to call themselves Christians but who are separated from one another, also as churches or communions, and from the church of Rome. The latter seeks a unity which, if it is to be the fruit and expression of true reconciliation, is meant to be based neither upon a disguising of the points that divide nor upon compromises which are as easy as they are superficial and fragile. Unity must be the result of a true conversion of everyone, the result of mutual forgiveness, of theological dialogue and fraternal relations, of prayer and of complete docility to the action of the Holy Spirit, who is also the Spirit of reconciliation.

Finally, in order that the church may say that she is completely reconciled, she feels that it is her duty to strive ever harder, by promoting the "dialogue of salvation,"[39] to bring the Gospel to those vast sections of humanity in the modern world that do not share her faith, but even, as a result of growing secularism, keep their distance from her and oppose her with cold indifference when they do not actually hinder and persecute her. She feels the duty to say once more to everyone in the words of St. Paul: "Be reconciled to God."[40]

At any rate, the church promotes reconciliation in the truth, knowing well that neither reconciliation nor unity is possible outside or in opposition to the truth.

3. God's Initiative and the Church's Ministry

10. The church, as a reconciled and reconciling community, cannot forget that at the source of her gift and mission of reconciliation is the initiative, full of compassionate love and mercy, of that God who is love[41] and who out of love created human beings;[42] and he created them so that they might live in friendship with him and in communion with one another.

Reconciliation Comes from God

God is faithful to his eternal plan even when man, under the impulse of the evil one[43] and carried away by his own pride, abuses the freedom given to him in order to love and generously seek what is good, and refuses to obey his Lord and Father. God is faithful even when man, instead of responding with love to God's love, opposes him and treats him like a rival, deluding himself and relying on his own power, with the resulting break of relationship with the one who created him. In spite of this transgression on man's part, God remains faithful in love. It is certainly true that the story of the Garden of Eden makes us think about the tragic consequences of rejecting the Father, which becomes evident in man's inner disorder and in the breakdown of harmony between man and woman, brother and brother.[44] Also significant is the gospel parable of the two brothers who, in different ways, distance themselves from their father and cause a rift between them. Refusal of God's fatherly love and of his loving gifts is always at the root of humanity's divisions.

But we know that God, "rich in mercy,"[45] like the father in the parable, does not close his heart to any of his children. He waits for them, looks for them, goes to meet them at the place where the refusal of communion imprisons them in isolation and division. He calls them to gather about his table in the joy of the feast of forgiveness and reconciliation.

This initiative on God's part is made concrete and manifest in the redemptive act of Christ, which radiates through the world by means of the ministry of the church.

For, according to our faith, the word of God became flesh and came to dwell in the world; he entered into the history of the world, summing it up and recapitulating it in himself.[46] He revealed to us that God is love, and he gave us the "new commandment" of love,[47] at the same time communicating to us the certainty that the path of love is open for all people, so that the effort to establish universal brotherhood is not a vain one.[48] By conquering through his death on the cross evil and the power of sin, by his loving obedience, he brought salvation to all and became "reconciliation" for all. In him God reconciled man to himself.

The church carries on the proclamation of reconciliation which Christ caused to echo through the villages of Galilee and all Palestine[49] and does not cease to invite all humanity to be converted and to believe in the good news. She speaks in the name of Christ, making her own the appeal of St. Paul which we have already recalled: "We are ambassadors for Christ, God making his appeal through us. We beseech you on behalf of Christ, be reconciled to God."[50]

Those who accept this appeal enter into the economy of reconciliation and experience the truth contained in that other affirmation of St. Paul, that Christ "is our peace, who has made us both one, and has broken down the dividing wall of hostility..., so making peace" that he "might reconcile us both to God."[51] This text directly concerns the overcoming of the religious division between Israel—as the chosen people of the Old Testament—and the other peoples, all called to form part of the new covenant. Nevertheless it contains the affirmation of the new spiritual universality desired by God and accomplished by him through the sacrifice of his Son, the word made man, without limits or exclusions of any sort, for all those who are converted and who believe in Christ. We are all therefore called to enjoy the fruits of this reconciliation desired by God: every individual and every people.

The Church, the Great Sacrament of Reconciliation

11. The church has the mission of proclaiming this reconciliation and as it were of being its sacrament in the world. The church is the sacrament, that is to say, the sign and means of reconciliation in different ways which differ in value but which all come together to obtain what the divine initiative of mercy desires to grant to humanity.

She is a sacrament in the first place by her very existence as a reconciled community which witnesses to and represents in the world the work of Christ.

She is also a sacrament through her service as the custodian and interpreter of sacred Scripture, which is the good news of reconciliation inasmuch as it tells each succeeding generation about God's loving plan and shows to each generation the paths to universal reconciliation in Christ.

Finally she is a sacrament by reason of the seven sacraments which, each in its own way, "make the church."[52] For since they commemorate and renew Christ's paschal mystery, all the sacraments are a source of life for the church and in the church's hands they are means of conversion to God and of reconciliation among people.

Other Means of Reconciliation

12. The mission of reconciliation is proper to the whole church, also and especially to that church which has already

been admitted to the full sharing in divine glory with the Virgin Mary, the angels and the saints, who contemplate and adore the thrice-holy God. The church in heaven, the church on earth and the church in purgatory are mysteriously united in this cooperation with Christ in reconciling the world to God.

The first means of this salvific action is that of prayer. It is certain that the Blessed Virgin, mother of Christ and of the church,[53] and the saints, who have now reached the end of their earthly journey and possess God's glory, sustain by their intercession their brethren who are on pilgrimage through the world, in the commitment to conversion, to faith, to getting up again after every fall, to acting in order to help the growth of communion and peace in the church and in the world. In the mystery of the communion of saints, universal reconciliation is accomplished in its most profound form, which is also the most fruitful for the salvation of all.

There is yet another means: that of preaching. The church, since she is the disciple of the one teacher Jesus Christ, in her own turn as mother and teacher untiringly exhorts people to reconciliation. And she does not hesitate to condemn the evil of sin, to proclaim the need for conversion, to invite and ask people to "let themselves be reconciled." In fact, this is her prophetic mission in today's world, just as it was in the world of yesterday. It is the same mission as that of her teacher and head, Jesus. Like him, the church will always carry out this mission with sentiments of merciful love and will bring to all people those words of for-giveness and that invitation to hope which come from the cross.

There is also the often so difficult and demanding means of pastoral action aimed at bringing back every individual—whoever and wherever he or she may be—to the path, at times a long one, leading back to the Father in the communion of all the brethren.

Finally there is the means of witness, which is almost always silent. This is born from a twofold awareness on the part of the church: that of being in herself "unfailingly holy,"[54] but also the awareness of the need to go forward and "daily be further purified and renewed, against the day when Christ will present her to himself in all her glory without spot or wrinkle," for, by reason of her sins, sometimes "the radiance of the church's face shines less brightly" in the eyes of those who behold her.[55] This witness cannot fail to assume two fundamental aspects. This first aspect is that of being the sign of that universal charity which Jesus Christ left as an inheritance to his followers, as a proof of belonging to his kingdom. The second aspect is translation into ever new manifestations of conversion and reconciliation both within the church and outside her, by the overcoming of tensions, by mutual forgiveness, by growth in the spirit of brotherhood and peace which is to be spread throughout the world. By this means the church will effectively be able to work for the creation of what my predecessor Paul VI called the "civilization of love."

Chapter II

The Love That Is Greater Than Sin

The Tragedy of Man

13. In the words of St. John the apostle, "If we say we have no sin, we deceive ourselves, and the truth is not in us. If we confess our sins, he is faithful and just and will forgive our sins."[56] Written at the very dawn of the church, these inspired words introduce better than any other human expression the theme of sin, which is intimately connected with that of reconciliation. These words present the question of sin in its human dimension: sin as an integral part of the truth about man. But they immediately relate the human dimension to its divine dimension, where sin is countered by the truth of divine love, which is just, generous and faithful, and which reveals itself above all in forgiveness and redemption. Thus St. John also writes a little further on that "whatever accusations (our conscience) may raise against us, God is greater than our conscience."[57]

To acknowledge one's sin, indeed—penetrating still more deeply into the consideration of one's own personhood—to recognize oneself as being a sinner, capable of sin and inclined to commit sin, is the essential first step in returning to God. For example, this is the experience of David, who "having done what is evil in the eyes of the Lord" and having been rebuked by the prophet Nathan,[58] exclaims: "For I know my transgressions, and my sin is ever before me. Against you, you alone, have I sinned and done what is evil in your sight."[59] Similarly, Jesus himself puts the following significant words on the lips and in the heart of the prodigal son: "Father, I have sinned against heaven and before you."[60]

In effect, to become reconciled with God presupposes and includes detaching oneself consciously and with determination from the sin into which one has fallen. It presupposes and includes, therefore, doing penance in the fullest sense of the term: repenting, showing this repentance, adopting a real attitude of repentance—which is the attitude of the person who starts out on the road of return to the Father. This is a general law and one which each individual must follow in his or her particular situation. For it is not possible to deal with sin and conversion only in abstract terms.

In the concrete circumstances of sinful humanity, in which there can be no conversion without the acknowledgment of one's own sin, the church's ministry of reconciliation intervenes in each individual case with a precise penitential purpose. That is, the church's ministry intervenes in order to bring the person to the "knowledge of self"—in the words of St. Catherine of Siena[61]—to the rejection of evil, to the re-establishment of friendship with God, to a new interior ordering, to a fresh ecclesial conversion. Indeed, even beyond the boundaries of the church and the community of believers, the message and ministry of penance are addressed to all men and women, because all need conversion and reconciliation.[62]

In order to carry out this penitential ministry adequately, we shall have to evaluate the consequences of sin with "eyes enlightened"[63] by faith. These consequences of sin are the reasons for division and rupture not only within each person, but also within the various circles of a person's life: in relation to the family, to the professional and social environment, as can often be seen from experience; it is confirmed by the passage in the Bible about the city of Babel and its tower.[64] Intent on building

32

what was to be at once a symbol and a source of unity, those people found themselves more scattered than before, divided in speech, divided among themselves, incapable of consensus and agreement.

Why did the ambitious project fail? Why did "the builders labor in vain?"[65] They failed because they had set up as a sign and guarantee of the unity they desired a work of their own hands alone and had forgotten the action of the Lord. They had attended only to the horizontal dimension of work and social life, forgetting the vertical dimension by which they would have been rooted in God, their creator and Lord, and would have been directed toward him as the ultimate goal of their progress.

Now it can be said that the tragedy of humanity today, as indeed of every period in history, consists precisely in its similarity to the experience of Babel.

1. The Mystery of Sin

14. If we read the passage in the Bible on the city and tower of Babel in the new light offered by the Gospel and if we compare it with the other passage on the fall of our first parents, we can draw from it valuable elements for an understanding of the mystery of sin. This expression, which echoes what St. Paul writes concerning the mystery of evil,[66] helps us to grasp the obscure and intangible element hidden in sin. Clearly sin is a product of man's freedom. But deep within its human reality there are factors at work which place it beyond the merely human, in the border area where man's conscience, will and sensitivity are in contact with the dark forces which, according to St. Paul, are active in the world almost to the point of ruling it.[67]

Disobedience to God

A first point which helps us to understand sin emerges from the biblical narrative on the building of the tower of Babel:

The people sought to build a city, organize themselves into a society and to be strong and powerful without God, if not precisely against God.[68] In this sense the story of the first sin in Eden and the story of Babel, in spite of notable differences in content and form, have one thing in common: In both there is an exclusion of God through direct opposition to one of his commandments, through an act of rivalry, through the mistaken pretension of being "like him."[69] In the story of Babel the exclusion of God is presented not so much under the aspect of opposition to him as of forgetfulness and indifference toward him, as if God were of no relevance in the sphere of man's joint projects. But in both cases the relationship to God is severed with violence. In the case of Eden there appears in all its seriousness and tragic reality that which constitutes the ultimate essence and darkness of sin: disobedience to God, to his law, to the moral norm that he has given man, inscribing it in his heart and confirming and perfecting it through revelation.

Exclusion of God, rupture with God, disobedience to God: Throughout the history of mankind this has been and is, in various forms, sin. It can go as far as a very denial of God and his existence: This is the phenomenon called atheism.

It is the disobedience of a person who, by a free act, does not acknowledge God's sovereignty over his or her life, at least at that particular moment in which he or she transgresses God's law.

Division Between Brothers

15. In the biblical narratives mentioned above, man's rupture with God leads tragically to divisions between brothers.

In the description of the "first sin," the rupture with Yahweh simultaneously breaks the bond of friendship that had united the human family. Thus the subsequent pages of Genesis show us the man and the woman as it were pointing an accusing finger at each other.[70] Later we have the brother hating his brother and finally taking his life.[71]

According to the Babel story, the result of sin is the shattering of the human family, already begun with the first sin and now reaching its most extreme form on the social level.

No one wishing to investigate the mystery of sin can ignore this link between cause and effect. As a rupture with God, sin is an act of disobedience by a creature who rejects, at least implicitly, the very one from whom he came and who sustains him in life. It is therefore a suicidal act. Since by sinning man refuses to submit to God, his internal balance is also destroyed and it is precisely within himself that contradictions and conflicts arise. Wounded in this way, man almost inevitably causes damage to the fabric of his relationship with others and with the created world. This is an objective law and an objective reality, verified in so many ways in the human psyche and in the spiritual life as well as in society, where it is easy to see the signs and effects of internal disorder.

The mystery of sin is composed of this twofold wound which the sinner opens in himself and in his relationship with his neighbor. Therefore one can speak of personal and social sin: From one point of view, every sin is personal; from another point of view, every sin is social insofar as and because it also has social repercussions.

Personal Sin and Social Sin

16. Sin, in the proper sense, is always a personal act, since it is an act of freedom on the part of an individual person and not properly of a group or community. This individual may be conditioned, incited and influenced by numerous and powerful external factors. He may also be subjected to tendencies, defects and habits linked with his personal condition. In not a few cases

such external and internal factors may attenuate, to a greater or lesser degree, the person's freedom and therefore his responsibility and guilt. But it is a truth of faith, also confirmed by our experience and reason, that the human person is free. This truth cannot be disregarded in order to place the blame for individuals' sins on external factors such as structures, systems or other people. Above all, this would be to deny the person's dignity and freedom, which are manifested—even though in a negative and disastrous way—also in this responsibility for sin committed. Hence there is nothing so personal and untransferable in each individual as merit for virtue or responsibility for sin.

As a personal act, sin has its first and most important consequences in the sinner himself: that is, in his relationship with God, who is the very foundation of human life; and also in his spirit, weakening his will and clouding his intellect.

At this point we must ask what was being referred to by those who during the preparation of the synod and in the course of its actual work frequently spoke of social sin.

The expression and the underlying concept in fact have various meanings.

To speak of social sin means in the first place to recognize that, by virtue of human solidarity which is as mysterious and intangible as it is real and concrete, each individual's sin in some way affects others. This is the other aspect of that solidarity which on the religious level is developed in the profound and magnificent mystery of the communion of saints, thanks to which it has been possible to say that "every soul that rises above itself, raises up the world."[72] To this law of ascent there unfortunately corresponds the law of descent. Consequently one can speak of a communion of sin, whereby a soul that lowers itself through sin drags down with itself the church and, in some way, the whole world. In other words, there is no sin, not even the most intimate and secret one, the most strictly individual one, that exclusively concerns the person committing it. With greater or lesser violence, with greater or lesser harm, every sin has repercussions on the entire ecclesial body and the whole human family. According to this first meaning of the term, every sin can undoubtedly be considered as social sin.

Some sins, however, by their very matter constitute a direct attack on one's neighbor and, more exactly, in the language of the Gospel, against one's brother or sister. They are an offense against God because they are offenses against one's neighbor. These sins are usually called social sins, and this is the second meaning of the term. In this sense social sin is sin against love of neighbor, and in the law of Christ it is all the more serious in that it involves the Second Commandment, which is "like unto the first."[73] Likewise, the term social applies to every sin against justice in interpersonal relationships, committed either by the individual against the community or by the community against the individual. Also social is every sin against the rights of the human person, beginning with the right to life and including the life of the unborn or against a person's physical integrity. Likewise social is every sin against others' freedom, especially against the supreme freedom to believe in God and adore him; social is every sin against the dignity and honor of one's neighbor. Also social is every sin against the common good and its exigencies in relation to the whole broad spectrum of the rights and duties of citizens. The term social can be applied to sins of commission or omission—on the part of political, economic or trade union leaders, who though in a position to do so, do not work diligently and wisely for the improvement and transformation of society according to the requirements and potential of the given historic moment; as also on the part of workers who through absenteeism or non-cooperation fail to ensure that their industries can continue to advance the well-being of the workers themselves, of their families and of the whole of society.

The third meaning of social sin refers to the relationships between the various human communities. These relationships are not always in accordance with the plan of God, who intends that there be justice in the world and freedom and peace between individuals, groups and peoples. Thus the class struggle, whoever the person who leads it or on occasion seeks to give it a theoretical justification, is a social evil. Likewise obstinate confrontation between blocs of nations, between one nation and another, between different groups within the same nation—all this too is a social evil. In both cases one may ask whether moral responsibility for these evils, and therefore sin, can be attributed to any person in particular. Now it has to be admitted that realities and situations such as those described, when they become generalized and reach vast proportions as social phenomena, almost always become anonymous, just as their causes are complex and not always identifiable. Hence if one speaks of social sin here, the expression obviously has an analogical meaning. However, to speak even analogically of social sins must not cause us to underestimate the responsibility of the individuals involved. It is meant to be an appeal to the consciences of all, so that each may shoulder his or her responsibility seriously and courageously in order to change those disastrous conditions and intolerable situations.

Having said this in the clearest and most unequivocal way, one must add at once that there is one meaning sometimes given to social sin that is not legitimate or acceptable even though it is very common in certain quarters today.[74] This usage contrasts social sin and personal sin, not without ambiguity, in a way that leads more or less unconsciously to the watering down and almost the abolition of personal sin, with the recognition only of social guilt and responsibilities. According to this usage, which can readily be seen to derive from non-Christian ideologies and systems—which have possibly been discarded today by the very people who formerly officially upheld them—practically every sin is a social sin, in the sense that blame for it is to be placed not so much on the moral conscience of an individual, but rather on some vague entity or anonymous collectivity such as the situation, the system, society, structures or institutions.

Whenever the church speaks of situations of sin or when she condemns as social sins certain situations or the collective behavior of certain social groups, big or small, or even of whole nations and blocs of nations, she knows and she proclaims that such cases of social sin are the result of the accumulation and concentration of many personal sins. It is a case of the very personal sins of those who cause or support evil or who exploit it; of those who are in a position to avoid, eliminate or at least limit certain social evils but who fail to do so out of laziness, fear or the conspiracy of silence, through secret complicity or indifference; of those who take refuge in the supposed impossibility of changing the world and also of those who sidestep the effort and sacrifice required, producing specious reasons of higher order. The real responsibility, then, lies with individuals.

A situation—or likewise an institution, a structure, society itself—is not in itself the subject of moral acts. Hence a situation cannot in itself be good or bad.

At the heart of every situation of sin are always to be found sinful people. So true is this that even when such a situation can be changed in its structural and institutional aspects by the force of law or—as unfortunately more often happens—by the law of force, the change in fact proves to be incomplete, of short duration and ultimately vain and ineffective—not to say counterproductive—if the people directly or indirectly responsible for that situation are not converted.

Mortal and Venial

17. But here we come to a further dimension in the mystery of sin, one on which the human mind has never ceased to ponder: the question of its gravity. It is a question which cannot be overlooked and one which the Christian conscience has never refused to answer. Why and to what degree is sin a serious

matter in the offense it commits against God and in its effects on man? The church has a teaching on this matter which she reaffirms in its essential elements, while recognizing that it is not always easy in concrete situations to define clear and exact limits.

Already in the Old Testament, individuals guilty of several kinds of sins—sins committed deliberately,[75] the various forms of impurity,[76] idolatry,[77] the worship of false gods[78]—were ordered to be "taken away from the people," which could also mean to be condemned to death.[79] Contrasted with these were other sins, especially sins committed through ignorance, that were forgiven by means of a sacrificial offering.[80]

In reference also to these texts, the church has for centuries spoken of mortal sin and venial sin. But it is above all the New Testament that sheds light on this distinction and these terms. Here there are many passages which enumerate and strongly reprove sins that are particularly deserving of condemnation.[81] There is also the confirmation of the Decalogue by Jesus himself.[82] Here I wish to give special attention to two passages that are significant and impressive.

In a text of his First Letter, St. John speaks of a sin which leads to death (pros thanaton), as opposed to a sin which does not lead to death (me pros thanaton).[83] Obviously, the concept of death here is a spiritual death. It is a question of the loss of the true life or "eternal life," which for John is knowledge of the Father and the Son,[84] and communion and intimacy with them. In that passage the sin that leads to death seems to be the denial of the Son[85] or the worship of false gods.[86] At any rate, by this distinction of concepts John seems to wish to emphasize the incalculable seriousness of what constitutes the very essence of sin, namely the rejection of God. This is manifested above all in apostasy and idolatry: repudiating faith in revealed truth and making certain created realities equal to God, raising them to the status of idols or false gods.[87] But in this passage the apostle's

40

intention is also to underline the certainty that comes to the Christian from the fact of having been "born of God" through the coming of the Son: The Christian possesses a power that preserves him from falling into sin; God protects him, and "the evil one does not touch him." If he should sin through weakness or ignorance, he has confidence in being forgiven, also because he is supported by the joint prayer of the community.

In another passage of the New Testament, namely in St. Matthew's Gospel,[88] Jesus himself speaks of a "blasphemy against the Holy Spirit" that "will not be forgiven" by reason of the fact that in its manifestations it is an obstinate refusal to be converted to the love of the Father of mercies.

Here of course it is a question of extreme and radical manifestations: rejection of God, rejection of his grace and therefore opposition to the very source of salvation[89]—these are manifestations whereby a person seems to exclude himself voluntarily from the path of forgiveness. It is to be hoped that very few persist to the end in this attitude of rebellion or even defiance of God. Moreover, God in his merciful love is greater than our hearts, as St. John further teaches us,[90] and can overcome all our psychological and spiritual resistance. So that, as St. Thomas writes, "considering the omnipotence and mercy of God, no one should despair of the salvation of anyone in this life."[91]

But when we ponder the problem of a rebellious will meeting the infinitely just God, we cannot but experience feelings of salutary "fear and trembling," as St. Paul suggests.[92] Moreover, Jesus' warning about the sin "that will not be forgiven" confirms the existence of sins which can bring down on the sinner the punishment of "eternal death."

In the light of these and other passages of sacred Scripture, doctors and theologians, spiritual teachers and pastors have divided sins into mortal and venial. St. Augustine, among others, speaks of *letalia* or *mortifera crimina*, contrasting them with *venialia, levia* or *quotidiana*.[93] The meaning which he gives to these adjectives was to influence the successive magisterium of the church. After him, it was St. Thomas who was to formulate in the clearest possible terms the doctrine which became a constant in the church.

In defining and distinguishing between mortal and venial sins, St. Thomas and the theology of sin that has its source in him could not be unaware of the biblical reference and therefore of the concept of spiritual death. According to St. Thomas, in order to live spiritually man must remain in communion with the supreme principle of life, which is God, since God is the ultimate end of man's being and acting. Now sin is a disorder perpetrated by man against this life principle. And when "through sin, the soul commits a disorder that reaches the point of turning away from its ultimate end—God—to which it is bound by charity, then the sin is mortal; on the other hand, whenever the disorder does not reach the point of a turning away from God, the sin is venial."[94] For this reason venial sin does not deprive the sinner of sanctifying grace, friendship with God, charity and therefore eternal happiness, whereas just such a deprivation is precisely the consequence of mortal sin.

Furthermore, when sin is considered from the point of view of the punishment it merits, for St. Thomas and other doctors mortal sin is the sin which, if unforgiven, leads to eternal punishment; whereas venial sin is the sin that merits merely temporal punishment (that is, a partial punishment which can be expiated on earth or in purgatory).

Considering sin from the point of view of its matter, the ideas of death, of radical rupture with God, the supreme good, of deviation from the path that leads to God or interruption of the journey toward him (which are all ways of defining mortal sin) are linked with the idea of the gravity of sin's objective content. Hence, in the church's doctrine and pastoral action, grave sin is in practice identified with mortal sin.

Here we have the core of the church's traditional teaching, which was reiterated frequently and vigorously during the recent synod. The synod in fact not only reaffirmed the teaching of the Council of Trent concerning the existence and nature of mortal and venial sins,[95] but it also recalled that mortal sin is sin whose object is grave matter and which is also committed with full knowledge and deliberate consent. It must be added—as was likewise done at the synod—that some sins are intrinsically grave and mortal by reason of their matter. That is, there exist acts which, *per se* and in themselves, independently of circumstances, are always seriously wrong by reason of their object. These acts, if carried out with sufficient awareness and freedom, are always gravely sinful.[96]

This doctrine, based on the Decalogue and on the preaching of the Old Testament, and assimilated into the *kerygma* of the apostles and belonging to the earliest teaching of the church, and constantly reaffirmed by her to this day, is exactly verified in the experience of the men and women of all times. Man knows well by experience that along the road of faith and justice which leads to the knowledge and love of God in this life and toward perfect union with him in eternity, he can cease to go forward or can go astray without abandoning the way of God; and in this case there occurs venial sin. This however must never be underestimated, as though it were automatically something that can be ignored or regarded as "a sin of little importance."

For man also knows, through painful experience, that by a conscious and free act of his will he can change course and go in a direction opposed to God's will, separating himself from God *(aversio a Deo)*, rejecting loving communion with him, detaching himself from the life principle which God is and consequently choosing death.

With the whole tradition of the church, we call mortal sin the act by which man freely and consciously rejects God, his law, the covenant of love that God offers, preferring to turn in on himself or to some created and finite reality, something contrary to the divine will *(conversio ad creaturam)*. This can occur in a direct and formal way in the sins of idolatry, apostasy and atheism; or in an equivalent way as in every act of disobedience to God's commandments in a grave matter. Man perceives that this disobedience to God destroys the bond that unites him with his life principle: It is a mortal sin, that is, an act which gravely offends God and ends in turning against man himself with a dark and powerful force of destruction.

During the synod assembly some fathers proposed a three-fold distinction of sins, classifying them as venial, grave and mortal. This threefold distinction might illustrate the fact that there is a scale of seriousness among grave sins. But it still remains true that the essential and decisive distinction is between sin which destroys charity and sin which does not kill the supernatural life: There is no middle way between life and death.

Likewise, care will have to be taken not to reduce mortal sin to an act of "fundamental option"—as is commonly said today—against God, intending thereby an explicit and formal contempt for God or neighbor. For mortal sin exists also when a person knowingly and willingly, for whatever reason, chooses something gravely disordered. In fact, such a choice already includes contempt for the divine law, a rejection of God's love for humanity and the whole of creation; the person turns away from God and loses charity. Thus the fundamental orientation can be radically changed by individual acts. Clearly there can occur situations which are very complex and obscure from a psychological viewpoint and which have an influence on the sinner's subjective culpability. But from a consideration of the psychological sphere one cannot proceed to the construction of a theological category, which is what the "fundamental option" precisely is, understanding it in such a way that it objectively changes or casts doubt upon the traditional concept of mortal sin.

While every sincere and prudent attempt to clarify the psychological and theological mystery of sin is to be valued, the church nevertheless has a duty to remind all scholars in this field of the need to be faithful to the word of God that teaches us also about sin. She likewise has to remind them of the risk of contributing to a further weakening of the sense of sin in the modern world.

The Loss of the Sense of Sin

18. Over the course of generations, the Christian mind has gained from the Gospel as it is read in the ecclesial community a fine sensitivity and an acute perception of the seeds of death contained in sin, as well as a sensitivity and an acuteness of perception for identifying them in the thousand guises under which sin shows itself. This is what is commonly called the sense of sin.

This sense is rooted in man's moral conscience and is as it were its thermometer. It is linked to the sense of God, since it derives from man's conscious relationship with God as his Creator, Lord and Father. Hence, just as it is impossible to eradicate completely the sense of God or to silence the conscience completely, so the sense of sin is never completely eliminated.

Nevertheless, it happens not infrequently in history, for more or less lengthy periods and under the influence of many different factors, that the moral conscience of many people becomes seriously clouded. "Have we the right idea of conscience?"—I asked two years ago in an address to the faithful—"Is it not true that modern man is threatened by an eclipse of conscience? By a deformation of conscience? By a numbness or 'deadening' of conscience?"[97] Too many signs indicate that such an eclipse exists in our time. This is all the more disturbing in that conscience, defined by the council as "the most secret core and sanctuary of a man,"[98] is "strictly related to human freedom....

45

For this reason conscience, to a great extent, constitutes the basis of man's interior dignity and, at the same time, of his relationship to God."[99] It is inevitable therefore that in this situation there is an obscuring also of the sense of sin, which is closely connected with the moral conscience, the search for truth and the desire to make a responsible use of freedom. When the conscience is weakened the sense of God is also obscured, and as a result, with the loss of this decisive inner point of reference, the sense of sin is lost. This explains why my predecessor Pius XII one day declared, in words that have almost become proverbial, that "the sin of the century is the loss of the sense of sin."[100]

Why has this happened in our time? A glance at certain aspects of contemporary culture can help us to understand the progressive weakening of the sense of sin, precisely because of the crisis of conscience and crisis of the sense of God already mentioned.

"Secularism" is by nature and definition a movement of ideas and behavior which advocates a humanism totally without God, completely centered upon the cult of action and production and caught up in the heady enthusiasm of consumerism and pleasure seeking, unconcerned with the danger of "losing one's soul." This secularism cannot but undermine the sense of sin. At the very most, sin will be reduced to what offends man. But it is precisely here that we are faced with the bitter experience which I already alluded to in my first encyclical, namely, that man can build a world without God, but this world will end by turning against him."[101] In fact, God is the origin and the supreme end of man, and man carries in himself a divine seed.[102] Hence it is the reality of God that reveals and illustrates the mystery of man. It is therefore vain to hope that there will take root a sense of sin against man and against human values, if there is no sense of offense against God, namely the true sense of sin.

Another reason for the disappearance of the sense of sin in

contemporary society is to be found in the errors made in evaluating certain findings of the human sciences. Thus on the basis of certain affirmations of psychology, concern to avoid creating feelings of guilt or to place limits on freedom leads to a refusal ever to admit any shortcoming. Through an undue extrapolation of the criteria of the science of sociology, it finally happens—as I have already said—that all failings are blamed upon society, and the individual is declared innocent of them. Again, a certain cultural anthropology so emphasizes the undeniable environmental and historical conditioning and influences which act upon man, that it reduces his responsibility to the point of not acknowledging his ability to perform truly human acts and therefore his ability to sin.

The sense of sin also easily declines as a result of a system of ethics deriving from a certain historical relativism. This may take the form of an ethical system which relativizes the moral norm, denying its absolute and unconditional value, and as a consequence denying that there can be intrinsically illicit acts independent of the circumstances in which they are performed by the subject. Herein lies a real "overthrowing and downfall of moral values," and "the problem is not so much one of ignorance of Christian ethics," but ignorance "rather of the meaning, foundations and criteria of the moral attitude."[103] Another effect of this ethical turning upside down is always such an attenuation of the notion of sin as almost to reach the point of saying that sin does exist, but no one knows who commits it.

Finally the sense of sin disappears when—as can happen in the education of youth, in the mass media and even in education within the family—it is wrongly identified with a morbid feeling of guilt or with the mere transgression of legal norms and precepts.

The loss of the sense of sin is thus a form or consequence of the denial of God: not only in the form of atheism but also in the form of secularism. If sin is the breaking off of one's filial

47

relationship to God in order to situate one's life outside of obedience to him, then to sin is not merely to deny God. To sin is also to live as if he did not exist, to eliminate him from one's daily life. A model of society which is mutilated or distorted in one sense or another, as is often encouraged by the mass media, greatly favors the gradual loss of the sense of sin. In such a situation the obscuring or weakening of the sense of sin comes from several sources: from a rejection of any reference to the transcendent in the name of the individual's aspiration to personal independence; from acceptance of ethical models imposed by general consensus and behavior, even when condemned by the individual conscience; from the tragic social and economic conditions that oppress a great part of humanity, causing a tendency to see errors and faults only in the context of society; finally and especially, from the obscuring of the notion of God's fatherhood and dominion over man's life.

Even in the field of the thought and life of the church certain trends inevitably favor the decline of the sense of sin. For example, some are inclined to replace exaggerated attitudes of the past with other exaggerations: From seeing sin everywhere they pass to not recognizing it anywhere; from too much emphasis on the fear of eternal punishment they pass to preaching a love of God that excludes any punishment deserved by sin; from severity in trying to correct erroneous consciences they pass to a kind of respect for conscience which excludes the duty of telling the truth. And should it not be added that the confusion caused in the consciences of many of the faithful by differences of opinions and teachings in theology, preaching, catechesis and spiritual direction on serious and delicate questions of Christian morals ends by diminishing the true sense of sin almost to the point of eliminating it altogether? Nor can certain deficiencies in the practice of sacramental penance be overlooked. These include the tendency to obscure the ecclesial significance of sin and of conversion and to reduce them to merely personal matters; or vice versa, the tendency to nullify the personal value of good and evil and to consider only their community dimension. There also exists the danger, never totally eliminated, of routine ritualism that deprives the sacrament of its full significance and formative effectiveness.

The restoration of a proper sense of sin is the first way of facing the grave spiritual crisis looming over man today. But the sense of sin can only be restored through a clear reminder of the unchangeable principles of reason and faith which the moral teaching of the church has always upheld.

There are good grounds for hoping that a healthy sense of sin will once again flourish, especially in the Christian world and in the church. This will be aided by sound catechetics, illuminated by the biblical theology of the covenant, by an attentive listening and trustful openness to the magisterium of the church, which never ceases to enlighten consciences, and by an ever more careful practice of the sacrament of penance.

2. "Mysterium Pietatis"

19. In order to understand sin we have had to direct our attention to its nature as made known to us by the revelation of the economy of salvation: This is the *mysterium iniquitatis.* But in this economy sin is not the main principle, still less the victor. Sin fights against another active principle which—to use a beautiful and evocative expression of St. Paul—we can call the *mysterium* or *sacramentum pietatis.* Man's sin would be the winner and in the end destructive, God's salvific plan would remain incomplete or even totally defeated, if this *mysterium pietatis* were not made part of the dynamism of history in order to conquer man's sin.

We find this expression in one of St. Paul's pastoral letters, the First Letter to Timothy. It appears unexpectedly, as if by an exuberant inspiration. The apostle had previously devoted long paragraphs of his message to his beloved disciple to an explanation of the meaning of the ordering of the community (the liturgical order and the related hierarchical one). Next he had spoken of the role of the heads of the community, before turning to the conduct of Timothy himself in "the church of the living God, the pillar and bulwark of the truth." Then at the end of the passage suddenly, but with a profound purpose, he evokes the element which gives meaning to everything that he has written: "Great indeed, we confess, is the mystery of our religion."[104]

Without in the least betraying the literal sense of the text, we can broaden this magnificent theological insight of St. Paul into a more complete vision of the role which the truth proclaimed by him plays in the economy of salvation: "Great indeed," we repeat with him, "is the mystery of our religion," because it conquers sin.

But what is the meaning of this expression, in Paul's mind?

It Is Christ Himself

20. It is profoundly significant that when Paul presents this *mysterium pietatis* he simply transcribes, without making a grammatical link with what he has just written,[105] three lines of a Christological hymn which—in the opinion of authoritative scholars—was used in the Greek-speaking Christian communities.

In the words of that hymn, full of theological content and rich in noble beauty, those first-century believers professed their faith in the mystery of Christ, whereby:

—He was made manifest in the reality of human flesh and was constituted by the Holy Spirit as the Just One who offers himself for the unjust.

—He appeared to the angels, having been made greater than them, and he was preached to the nations as the bearer of salvation.

—He was believed in, in the world, as the one sent by the

Father, and by the same Father assumed into heaven as Lord.[106]

The mystery or sacrament of *pietas*, therefore, is the very mystery of Christ. It is, in a striking summary, the mystery of the incarnation and redemption, of the full passover of Jesus, the Son of God and son of Mary: the mystery of his passion and death, of his resurrection and glorification. What St. Paul in quoting the phrases of the hymn wished to emphasize was that this mystery is the hidden vital principle which makes the church the house of God, the pillar and bulwark of the truth. Following the Pauline teaching, we can affirm that this same mystery of God's infinite loving kindness toward us is capable of penetrating to the hidden roots of our iniquity, in order to evoke in the soul a movement of conversion, in order to redeem it and set it on course toward reconciliation.

St. John too undoubtedly referring to this mystery, but in his own characteristic language which differs from St. Paul's, was able to write that "anyone born of God does not sin, but he who was born of God keeps him, and the evil one does not touch him."[107] In this Johannine affirmation there is an indication of hope, based on the divine promises: The Christian has received the guarantee and the necessary strength not to sin. It is not a question therefore of a sinlessness acquired through one's own virtue or even inherent in man, as the Gnostics thought. It is a result of God's action. In order not to sin the Christian has knowledge of God, as St. John reminds us in this same passage. But a little before he had written: "No one born of God commits sin; for God's seed abides in him."[108] If by "God's seed" we understand, as some commentators suggest, Jesus the Son of God, then we can say that in order not to sin or in order to gain freedom from sin the Christian has within himself the presence of Christ and the mystery of Christ, which is the mystery of God's loving kindness.

The Effort of the Christian

21. But there is another aspect to *the mysterium pietatis:* The loving kindness of God toward the Christian must be matched by the piety of the Christian toward God. In this second meaning of the word, piety *(eusebeia)* means precisely the conduct of the Christian who responds to God's fatherly loving kindness with his own filial piety.

In this sense too we can say with St. Paul that "great indeed is the mystery of our religion." In this sense too piety, as a force for conversion and reconciliation, confronts iniquity and sin. In this case too the essential aspects of the mystery of Christ are the object of piety in the sense that the Christian accepts the mystery, contemplates it and draws from it the spiritual strength necessary for living according to the Gospel. Here too one must say that "no one born of God commits sin"; but the expression has an imperative sense: Sustained by the mystery of Christ as by an interior source of spiritual energy, the Christian, being a child of God, is warned not to sin and indeed receives the commandment not to sin but to live in a manner worthy of "the house of God, that is, the church of the living God."[109]

Toward a Reconciled Life

22. Thus the word of Scripture, as it reveals to us the mystery of *pietas,* opens the intellect to conversion and reconciliation, understood not as lofty abstractions but as concrete Christian values to be achieved in our daily lives.

Deceived by the loss of the sense of sin and at times tempted by an illusion of sinlessness which is not at all Christian, the people of today too need to listen again to St. John's admonition, as addressed to each one of them personally: "If we say we have no sin, we deceive ourselves, and the truth is not in us,"[110] and indeed, "the whole world is in the power of the evil one."[111] Every individual therefore is invited by the voice of divine truth to examine realistically his or her conscience and to confess that he or she has been brought forth in iniquity, as we say in the *Miserere* psalm."[112]

Nevertheless, though threatened by fear and despair, the people of today can feel uplifted by the divine promise which opens to them the hope of full reconciliation.

The mystery of *pietas*, on God's part, is that mercy in which our Lord and Father—I repeat it again—is infinitely rich.[113] As I said in my encyclical on the subject of divine mercy,[114] it is a love more powerful than sin, stronger than death. When we realize that God's love for us does not cease in the face of our sin or recoil before our offenses, but becomes even more attentive and generous; when we realize that this love went so far as to cause the passion and death of the Word made flesh who consented to redeem us at the price of his own blood, then we exclaim in gratitude: "Yes, the Lord is rich in mercy," and even: "The Lord is mercy."

The mystery of *pietas* is the path opened by divine mercy to a reconciled life.

Chapter III

The Pastoral Ministry
of Penance and Reconciliation

Promoting Penance and Reconciliation

23. To evoke conversion and penance in man's heart and to
offer him the gift of reconciliation is the specific mission of the
church as she continues the redemptive work of her divine
founder. It is not a mission which consists merely of a few
theoretical statements and the putting forward of an ethical ideal
unaccompanied by the energy with which to carry it out. Rather
it seeks to express itself in precise ministerial functions directed
toward a concrete practice of penance and reconciliation.

We can call this ministry, which is founded on and illu-
mined by the principles of faith which we have explained and
which is directed toward precise objectives and sustained by
adequate means, the pastoral activity of penance and reconciliation. Its point of departure is the church's conviction that man,
to whom every form of pastoral activity is directed but principally that of penance and reconciliation, is the man marked by
sin whose striking image is to be found in King David. Rebuked
by the prophet Nathan, David faces squarely his own iniquity
and confesses: "I have sinned against the Lord,"[115] and proclaims: "I know my transgressions, and my sin is ever before
me."[116] But he also prays: "Purge me with hyssop, and I shall be
clean; wash me, and I shall be whiter than snow,"[117] and he
receives the response of the divine mercy: "The Lord has put

away your sin; you shall not die." [118]

The church thus finds herself face to face with man—with the whole human world—wounded by sin and affected by sin in the innermost depths of his being. But at the same time he is moved by an unrestrainable desire to be freed from sin and, especially if he is a Christian, he is aware that the mystery of *pietas,* Christ the Lord, is already acting in him and in the world by the power of the redemption.

The church's reconciling role must therefore be carried out in accordance with that intimate link which closely connects the forgiveness and remission of the sin of each person with the fundamental and full reconciliation of humanity which took place with the redemption. This link helps us to understand that, since sin is the active principle of division—division between man and the nature created by God—only conversion from sin is capable of bringing about a profound and lasting reconciliation wherever division has penetrated.

I do not need to repeat what I have already said about the importance of this "ministry of reconciliation,"[119] and of the pastoral activity whereby it is carried out in the church's consciousness and life. This pastoral activity would be lacking an essential aspect of its being and failing in an indispensable function if the "message of reconciliation"[120] were not proclaimed with clarity and tenacity in season and out of season, and if the gift of reconciliation were not offered to the world. But it is worth repeating that the importance of the ecclesial service of reconciliation extends beyond the confines of the church to the whole world.

To speak of the pastoral activity of penance and reconciliation, then, is to refer to all the tasks incumbent on the church, at all levels, for their promotion. More concretely, to speak of this pastoral activity is to evoke all the activities whereby the church, through each and every one of her members—pastors and faithful, at all levels and in all spheres, and with all the means at her disposal, words and actions, teaching and prayer—leads people individually or as groups to true penance and thus sets them on the path to full reconciliation.

The fathers of the synod, as representatives of their brother bishops and as leaders of the people entrusted to them, concerned themselves with the most practical and concrete elements of this pastoral activity. And I am happy to echo their concerns by associating myself with their anxieties and hopes, by receiving the results of their research and experiences, and by encouraging them in their plans and achievements. May they find in this part of the present apostolic exhortation the contribution which they themselves made to the synod, a contribution the usefulness of which I wish to extend, through these pages, to the whole church.

I therefore propose to call attention to the essentials of the pastoral activity of penance and reconciliation by emphasizing, with the synod assembly, the following two points:

1. The means used and the paths followed by the church in order to promote penance and reconciliation.

2. The sacrament *par excellence* of penance and reconciliation.

1. The Promotion of Penance and Reconciliation: Ways and Means

24. In order to promote penance and reconciliation, the church has at her disposal two principal means which were entrusted to her by her founder himself: catechesis and the sacraments. Their use has always been considered by the church as fully in harmony with the requirements of her salvific mission and at the same time as corresponding to the requirements and spiritual needs of people in all ages. This use can be in forms and ways both old and new, among which it will be a good idea to remember in particular what we can call, in the expression of my predecessor Paul VI, the method of dialogue.

Dialogue

25. For the church, dialogue is in a certain sense a means and especially a way of carrying out her activity in the modern world.

The Second Vatican Council proclaims that "the church, by virtue of her mission to shed on the whole world the radiance of the gospel message, and to unify under one Spirit all people... stands forth as a sign of that fraternal solidarity which allows honest dialogue and invigorates it." The council adds that the church should be capable of "establishing an ever more fruitful dialogue among all those who compose the one people of God"[121] and also of "establishing a dialogue with human society."[122]

My predecessor Paul VI devoted to dialogue a considerable part of his first encyclical, *Ecclesism Suam*, in which he describes it and significantly characterizes it as the dialogue of salvation.[123]

The church in fact uses the method of dialogue in order the better to lead people—both those who through baptism and the profession of faith acknowledge their membership of the Christian community and also those who are outside—to conversion and repentance, along the path of a profound renewal of their own consciences and lives in the light of the mystery of the redemption and salvation accomplished by Christ and entrusted to the ministry of his church. Authentic dialogue, therefore, is aimed above all at the rebirth of individuals through interior conversion and repentance, but always with profound respect for consciences and with patience and at the step-by-step pace indispensable for modern conditions.

Pastoral dialogue aimed at reconciliation continues to be today a fundamental task of the church in different spheres and at different levels.

The church in the first place promotes an ecumenical dialogue, that is, with churches and ecclesial communities which profess faith in Christ, the Son of God and only savior. She also promotes dialogue with the other communities of people who are seeking God and wish to have a relationship of communion with him.

At the basis of this dialogue with the other churches and Christian communities and with the other religions, and as a condition of her credibility and effectiveness, there must be a sincere effort of permanent and renewed dialogue within the Catholic Church herself. She is aware that, by her nature, she is the sacrament of the universal communion of charity;[124] but she is equally aware of the tensions within her, tensions which risk becoming factors of division.

The heartfelt and determined invitation which was already extended by my predecessor in preparation for the 1975 Holy Year[125] is also valid at the present moment. In order to overcome conflicts and to ensure that normal tensions do not prove harmful to the unity of the church, we must all apply to ourselves the word of God; we must relinquish our own subjective views and seek the truth where it is to be found, namely in the divine word itself and in the authentic interpretation of that word provided by the magisterium of the church. In this light, listening to one another, respect, refraining from all hasty judgments, patience, the ability to avoid subordinating the faith which unites to the opinions, fashions and ideological choices which divide—these are all qualities of a dialogue within the church which must be persevering, open and sincere. Obviously dialogue would not have these qualities and would not become a factor of reconciliation if the magisterium were not heeded and accepted.

Thus actively engaged in seeking her own internal communion, the Catholic Church can address an appeal for reconciliation to the other churches with which there does not exist full communion, as well as to the other religions and even to all those who are seeking God with a sincere heart. This she has been doing for some time.

In the light of the council and of the magisterium of my predecessors, whose precious inheritance I have received and am making every effort to preserve and put into effect, I can affirm that the Catholic Church at every level is committed to frank ecumenical dialogue, without facile optimism but also without distrust and without hesitation or delays. The fundamental laws which she seeks to follow in this dialogue are, on the one hand, the conviction that only a spiritual ecumenism—namely an ecumenism founded on common prayer and in a common docility to the one Lord—enables us to make a sincere and serious response to the other exigencies of ecumenical action.[126] The other law is the conviction that a certain facile irenicism in doctrinal and especially dogmatic matters could perhaps lead to a form of superficial and short-lived coexistence, but it could not lead to that profound and stable communion which we all long for. This communion will be reached at the hour willed by divine providence. But in order to reach it, the Catholic Church, for her part, knows that she must be open and sensitive to all "the truly Christian endowments from our common heritage which are to be found among our separated brethren";[127] but she also knows that she must likewise base a frank and constructive dialogue upon a clarity regarding her own positions and upon fidelity and consistency with the faith transmitted and defined in accordance with the perennial tradition of her magisterium. Notwithstanding the threat of a certain defeatism and despite the inevitable slowness which rashness could never correct, the Catholic Church continues with all other Christian brethren to seek the paths to unity, and with the followers of the other religions she continues to seek to have sincere dialogue. May this inter-religious dialogue lead to the overcoming of all attitudes of hostility, distrust, mutual condemnation and even mutual invective, which is the precondition for encounter at least in faith in one God and in the certainty of eternal life for the immortal soul. May the Lord especially grant that ecumenical dialogue will also lead to a sincere reconciliation concerning everything that we already have in common with the other Christian churches: faith in Jesus Christ, the Son of God made man, our savior and Lord; a listening to the word; the study of revelation and the sacrament of baptism.

To the extent to which the church is capable of generating active harmony—unity in variety—within herself and of offering herself as a witness to and humble servant of reconciliation with the other churches and ecclesial communities and the other religions, she becomes, in the expressive definition of St. Augustine, a "reconciled world."[128] Then she will be able to be a sign of reconciliation in the world and for the world.

The church is aware of the extreme seriousness of the situation created by the forces of division and war, which today constitute a grave threat not only to the balance and harmony of nations but to the very survival of humanity, and she feels it her duty to offer and suggest her own unique collaboration for the overcoming of conflicts and the restoration of concord.

It is a complex and delicate dialogue of reconciliation in which the church is engaged, especially through the work of the Holy See and its different organisms. The Holy See already endeavors to intervene with the leaders of nations and the heads of the various international bodies or seeks to associate itself with them, conduct a dialogue with them and encourage them to dialogue with one another for the sake of reconciliation in the midst of the many conflicts. It does this not for ulterior motives or hidden interests—since it has none—but "out of a humanitarian concern,"[129] placing its institutional structure and moral authority, which are altogether unique, at the service of concord and peace. It does this in the conviction that as "in war two parties rise against one another" so "in the question of peace there are also necessarily two parties which must know how to commit themselves," and in this "one finds the true meaning of a dialogue for peace."[130]

The church engages in dialogue for reconciliation also through the bishops in the competency and responsibility proper to them, either individually in the direction of their respective local churches or united in their episcopal conferences, with the collaboration of the priests and of all those who make up the Christian communities. They truly fulfill their task when they promote this indispensable dialogue and proclaim the human and Christian need for reconciliation and peace. In communion with their pastors, the laity who have as "their own field of evangelizing activity...the vast and complicated world of politics, society...economics...(and) international life,"[131] are called upon to engage directly in dialogue or to work for dialogue aimed at reconciliation. Through them too the church carries out her reconciling activity. Thus the fundamental presupposition and secure basis for any lasting renewal of society and for peace between nations lies in the regeneration of hearts through conversion and penance.

It should be repeated that, on the part of the church and her members, dialogue, whatever form it takes (and these forms can be and are very diverse since the very concept of dialogue has an analogical value) can never begin from an attitude of indifference to the truth. On the contrary, it must begin from a presentation of the truth, offered in a calm way, with respect for the intelligence and consciences of others. The dialogue of reconciliation can never replace or attenuate the proclamation of the truth of the Gospel, the precise goal of which is conversion from sin and communion with Christ and the church. It must be at the service of the transmission and realization of that truth through the means left by Christ to the church for the pastoral activity of reconciliation, namely catechesis and penance.

Catechesis

26. In the vast area in which the church has the mission of operating through dialogue, the pastoral ministry of penance

and reconciliation is directed to the members of the body of the church principally through an adequate catechesis concerning the two distinct and complementary realities to which the synod fathers gave a particular importance and which they emphasized in some of the concluding propositiones: These are penance and reconciliation. Catechesis is therefore the first means to be used.

At the basis of the synod's very opportune recommendation is a fundamental presupposition: What is pastoral is not opposed to what is doctrinal. Nor can pastoral action prescind from doctrinal content, from which in fact it draws its substance and real validity. Now if the church is the "pillar and bulwark of the truth"[132] and is placed in the world as mother and teacher, how could she neglect the task of teaching the truth which constitutes a path of life?

From the pastors of the church one expects, first of all, catechesis on reconciliation. This must be founded on the teaching of the Bible, especially the New Testament, on the need to rebuild the covenant with God in Christ the redeemer and reconciler. And in the light of this new communion and friendship, and as an extension of it, it must be founded on the teaching concerning the need to be reconciled with one's brethren, even if this means interrupting the offering of the sacrifice.[133] Jesus strongly insists on this theme of fraternal reconciliation: for example, when he invites us to turn the other cheek to the one who strikes us, and to give our cloak too to the one who has taken our coat,[134] or when he instills the law of forgiveness: forgiveness which each one receives in the measure that he or she forgives,[135] forgiveness to be offered even to enemies,[136] forgiveness to be granted seventy times seven times,[137] which means in practice without any limit. On these conditions, which are realizable only in a genuinely evangelical climate, it is possible to have a true reconciliation between individuals, families, communities, nations and peoples. From these biblical data on reconciliation there will naturally derive a theological catechesis, which in its synthesis will also integrate the elements of psychology, sociology and the other human sciences which can serve to clarify situations, describe problems accurately and persuade listeners or readers to make concrete resolutions.

The pastors of the church are also expected to provide catechesis on penance. Here too the richness of the biblical message must be its source. With regard to penance this message emphasizes particularly its value for conversion, which is the term that attempts to translate the word in the Greek text, *metanoia*,[138] which literally means to allow the spirit to be overturned in order to make it turn toward God. These are also the two fundamental elements which emerge from the parable of the son who was lost and found: his "coming to himself"[139] and his decision to return to his father. There can be no reconciliation unless these attitudes of conversion come first, and catechesis should explain them with concepts and terms adapted to people's various ages and their differing cultural, moral and social backgrounds.

This is a first value of penance and it extends into a second: Penance also means repentance. The two meanings of *metanoia* appear in the significant instruction given by Jesus: "If your brother repents (returns to you), forgive him; and if he sins against you seven times in the day, and turns to you seven times and says, 'I repent,' you must forgive him."[140] A good catechesis will show how repentance, just like conversion, is far from being a superficial feeling but a real overturning of the soul.

A third value is contained in penance, and this is the movement whereby the preceding attitudes of conversion and repentance are manifested externally: This is doing penance. This meaning is clearly perceptible in the term *metanoia*, as used by John the Baptist in the texts of the synoptics.[141] To do penance means above all to re-establish the balance and harmony broken by sin, to change direction even at the cost of sacrifice.

A catechesis on penance, therefore, and one that is as complete and adequate as possible, is absolutely essential at a time like ours when dominant attitudes in psychology and social behavior are in such contrast with the threefold value just illustrated. Contemporary man seems to find it harder than ever to recognize his own mistakes and to decide to retrace his steps and begin again after changing course. He seems very reluctant to say "I repent" or "I am sorry." He seems to refuse instinctively and often irresistibly anything that is penance in the sense of a sacrifice accepted and carried out for the correction of sin. In this regard I would like to emphasize that the church's penitential discipline, even though it has been mitigated for some time, cannot be abandoned without grave harm both to the interior life of individual Christians and of the ecclesial community and also to their capacity for missionary influence. It is not uncommon for non-Christians to be surprised at the negligible witness of true penance on the part of Christ's followers. It is clear, however, that Christian penance will only be authentic if it is inspired by love and not by mere fear; if it consists in a serious effort to crucify the "old man" so that the "new" can be born by the power of Christ; if it takes as its model Christ, who though he was innocent chose the path of poverty, patience, austerity and, one can say, the penitential life.

As the synod recalled, the pastors of the church are also expected to provide catechesis on conscience and its formation. This too is a very relevant topic in view of the fact that in the upheavals to which our present culture is subjected this interior sanctuary, man's innermost self, his conscience, is too often attacked, put to the test, confused and obscured. Valuable guidelines for a wise catechesis on conscience can be found both in the doctors of the church and in the theology of the Second Vatican Council, and especially in the documents on the church in the modern world[142] and on religious liberty.[143] Along these same lines, Pope Paul VI often reminded us of the nature and role of conscience in our life.[144] I myself, following his footsteps, miss no opportunity to throw light on this most lofty element of man's greatness and dignity,[145] this "sort of moral sense which leads us to discern what is good and what is evil...like an inner eye, a visual capacity of the spirit, able to guide our steps along the path of good." And I have reiterated the need to form one's conscience, lest it become "a force which is destructive of the true humanity of the person, rather than that holy place where God reveals to him his true good."[146]

On other points too, of no less relevance for reconciliation, one looks to the pastors of the church for catechesis.

On the sense of sin, which, as I have said, has become considerably weakened in our world.

On temptation and temptations: The Lord Jesus himself, the Son of God, "who in every respect has been tempted as we are, yet without sin,"[147] allowed himself to be tempted by the evil one[148] in order to show that, like himself, his followers too would be subjected to temptation, and in order to show how one should behave when subjected to temptation. For those who beseech the Father not to be tempted beyond their own strength[149] and not to succumb to temptation,[150] and for those who do not expose themselves to occasions of sin, being subjected to temptation does not mean that they have sinned; rather it is an opportunity for growing in fidelity and consistency through humility and watchfulness.

Catechesis is also expected on fasting: This can be practiced in old forms and new as a sign of conversion, repentance and personal mortification and, at the same time, as a sign of union with Christ crucified and of solidarity with the starving and suffering.

Catechesis on almsgiving: This is a means of making charity a practical thing by sharing what one possesses with those suffering the consequences of poverty.

Catechesis on the intimate connection which links the

overcoming of divisions in the world with perfect communion with God and among people, which is the eschatological purpose of the church.

Catechesis on the concrete circumstances in which reconciliation has to be achieved (in the family, in the civil community, in social structures) and particularly catechesis on the four reconciliations which repair the four fundamental rifts: reconciliation of man with God, with self, with the brethren and with the whole of creation.

Nor can the church omit, without serious mutilation of her essential message, a constant catechesis on what the traditional Christian language calls the four last things of man: death, judgment (universal and particular), hell and heaven. In a culture which tends to imprison man in the earthly life at which he is more or less successful, the pastors of the church are asked to provide a catechesis which will reveal and illustrate with the certainties of faith what comes after the present life: beyond the mysterious gates of death, an eternity of joy in communion with God or the punishment of separation from him. Only in this eschatological vision can one realize the exact nature of sin and feel decisively moved to penance and reconciliation.

Pastors who are zealous and creative never lack opportunities for imparting this broad and varied catechesis, taking into account the different degrees of education and religious formation of those to whom they speak. Such opportunities are often given by the biblical readings and the rites of the Mass and the sacraments, as also by the circumstances of their celebration. For the same purpose many initiatives can be taken such as sermons, lectures, discussions, meetings, courses of religious education, etc., as happens in many places. Here I wish to point out in particular the importance and effectiveness of the old-style popular missions for the purposes of such catechesis. If adapted to the peculiar needs of the present time, such missions can be, today as yesterday, a useful instrument of religious education also regarding penance and reconciliation.

In view of the great relevance of reconciliation based on conversion in the delicate field of human relationships and social interaction at all levels, including the international level, catechesis cannot fail to inculcate the valuable contribution of the church's social teaching. The timely and precise teaching of my predecessors from Pope Leo XIII onward, to which was added the substantial contribution of the pastoral constitution *Gaudium et Spes* of the Second Vatican Council and the contributions of the different episcopates elicited by various circumstances in their respective countries, has made up an ample and solid body of doctrine. This regards the many different needs inherent in the life of the human community, in relationships between individuals, families, groups in their different spheres and in the very constitution of a society that intends to follow the moral law, which is the foundation of civilization.

At the basis of this social teaching of the church there is obviously to be found the vision which the church draws from the word of God concerning the rights and duties of individuals, the family and the community; concerning the value of liberty and the nature of justice, concerning the primacy of charity, concerning the dignity of the human person and the exigencies of the common good to which politics and the economy itself must be directed. Upon these fundamental principles of the social magisterium, which confirm and repropose the universal dictates of reason and of the conscience of peoples, there rests in great part the hope for a peaceful solution to many social conflicts and, in short, the hope for universal reconciliation.

The Sacraments

27. The second divinely instituted means which the church offers for the pastoral activity of penance and reconciliation is constituted by the sacraments.

In the mysterious dynamism of the sacraments, so rich in

symbolism and content, one can discern one aspect which is not always emphasized: Each sacrament, over and above its own proper grace, is also a sign of penance and reconciliation. Therefore in each of them it is possible to relive these dimensions of the spirit.

Baptism is of course a salvific washing which, as St. Peter says, is effective "not as a removal of dirt from the body but as an appeal to God for a clear conscience."[151] It is death, burial and resurrection with the dead, buried and risen Christ.[152] It is a gift of the Holy Spirit through Christ.[153] But this essential and original constituent of Christian baptism, far from eliminating the penitential element already present in the baptism which Jesus himself received from John "to fulfill all righteousness,"[154] in fact enriches it. In other words, it is a fact of conversion and of reintegration into the right order of relationships with God, of reconciliation with God, with the elimination of the original stain and the consequent introduction into the great family of the reconciled.

Confirmation likewise, as a ratification of baptism and together with baptism a sacrament of initiation, in conferring the fullness of the Holy Spirit and in bringing the Christian life to maturity, signifies and accomplishes thereby a greater conversion of the heart and brings about a more intimate and effective membership of the same assembly of the reconciled, which is the church of Christ.

The definition which St. Augustine gives of the eucharist as *"sacramentum pietatis, signum unitatis, vinculum caritatis"*[155] clearly illustrates the effects of personal sanctification *(pietas)* and community reconciliation *(unitas and caritas)* which derive from the very essence of the eucharistic mystery as an unbloody renewal of the sacrifice of the cross, the source of salvation and of reconciliation for all people.

However, it must be remembered that the church, guided by faith in this great sacrament, teaches that no Christian who is conscious of grave sin can receive the eucharist before having obtained God's forgiveness. This we read in the instruction *Eucharisticum Mysterium* which, duly approved by Paul VI, fully confirms the teaching of the Council of Trent: "The eucharist is to be offered to the faithful also 'as a remedy, which frees us from daily faults and preserves us from mortal sin' and they are to be shown the fitting way of using the penitential parts of the liturgy of the Mass. The person who wishes to receive holy communion is to be reminded of the precept: 'Let a man examine himself' (1 Cor 11:28). And the church's custom shows that such an examination is necessary, because no one who is conscious of being in mortal sin, however contrite he may believe himself to be, is to approach the holy eucharist without having first made a sacramental confession. If this person finds himself in need and has no means of going to confession, he should first make an act of perfect contrition."[156]

The sacrament of orders is intended to give to the church the pastors who, besides being teachers and guides, are called to be witnesses and workers of unity, builders of the family of God, and defenders and preservers of the communion of this family against the sources of division and dispersion.

The sacrament of matrimony, the exaltation of human love under the action of grace, is a sign of the love of Christ for the church. But it is also a sign of the victory which Christ grants to couples in resisting the forces which deform and destroy love, in order that the family born from this sacrament may be a sign also of the reconciled and reconciling church for a world reconciled in all its structures and institutions.

Finally, the anointing of the sick in the trial of illness and old age and especially at the Christian's final hour is a sign of definitive conversion to the Lord and of total acceptance of suffering and death as a penance for sins. And in this is accomplished supreme reconciliation with the Father.

However, among the sacraments there is one which, though

it has often been called the sacrament of confession because of the accusation of sins which takes place in it, can more appropriately be considered by antonomasia the sacrament of penance, as it is in fact called. And thus it is the sacrament of conversion and reconciliation. The recent synod particularly concerned itself with this sacrament because of its importance with regard to reconciliation.

2. The Sacrament of Penance and Reconciliation

28. In all its phases and at all its levels the synod considered with the greatest attention that sacramental sign which represents and at the same time accomplishes penance and reconciliation. This sacrament in itself certainly does not contain all possible ideas of conversion and reconciliation. From the very beginning, in fact, the church has recognized and used many and varying forms of penance. Some are liturgical or paraliturgical and include the penitential act in the Mass, services of atonement and pilgrimages; others are of an ascetical character, such as fasting. But of all such acts none is more significant, more divinely efficacious or more lofty and at the same time easily accessible as a rite than the sacrament of penance.

From its preparatory stage and then in the numerous interventions during the sessions, in the group meetings and in the final *propositiones,* the synod took into account the statement frequently made with varying nuances and emphases, namely: The sacrament of penance is in crisis. The synod took note of this crisis. It recommended a more profound catechesis, but it also recommended a no less profound analysis of a theological, historical, psychological, sociological and juridical character of penance in general and of the sacrament of penance in particular. In all of this the synod's intention was to clarify the reasons for the crisis and to open the way to a positive solution for the good of humanity. Meanwhile, from the synod itself the church has received a clear confirmation of its faith regarding the sacrament which gives to every Christian and to the whole community of believers the certainty of forgiveness through the power of the redeeming blood of Christ.

It is good to renew and reaffirm this faith at a moment when it might be weakening, losing something of its completeness or entering into an area of shadow and silence, threatened as it is by the negative elements of the above-mentioned crisis. For the sacrament of confession is indeed being undermined, on the one hand by the obscuring of the moral and religious conscience, the lessening of a sense of sin, the distortion of the concept of repentance and the lack of effort to live an authentically Christian life. And on the other hand, it is being undermined by the sometimes widespread idea that one can obtain forgiveness directly from God, even in a habitual way, without approaching the sacrament of reconciliation. A further negative influence is the routine of a sacramental practice sometimes lacking in fervor and real spontaneity, deriving perhaps from a mistaken and distorted idea of the effects of the sacrament.

It is therefore appropriate to recall the principal aspects of this great sacrament.

"Whose Sins You Shall Forgive"

29. The books of the Old and New Testament provide us with the first and fundamental fact concerning the Lord's mercy and forgiveness. In the Psalms and in the preaching of the prophets, the name merciful is perhaps the one most often given to the Lord, in contrast to the persistent cliche whereby the God of the Old Testament is presented above all as severe and vengeful. Thus in the Psalms there is a long sapiential passage drawing from the Exodus tradition, which recalls God's kindly action in the midst of his people. This action, though represented in an anthropomorphic way, is perhaps one of the most eloquent Old Testament proclamations of the divine mercy. Suffice it to

quote the verse: "Yet he, being compassionate, forgave their iniquity and did not destroy them; he restrained his anger often, and did not stir up all his wrath. He remembered that they were but flesh, a wind that passes and comes not again."[157]

In the fullness of time the Son of God, coming as the lamb who takes away and bears upon himself the sin of the world,[158] appears as the one who has the power both to judge[159] and to forgive sins,[160] and who has come not to condemn but to forgive and save.[161]

Now this power to "forgive sins" Jesus confers through the Holy Spirit upon ordinary men, themselves subject to the snare of sin, namely his apostles: "Receive the Holy Spirit. Whose sins you shall forgive, they are forgiven; whose sins you shall retain, they are retained."[162] This is one of the most awe-inspiring innovations of the Gospel! He confers this power on the apostles also as something which they can transmit—as the church has understood it from the beginning—to their successors, charged by the same apostles with the mission and responsibility of continuing their work as proclaimers of the Gospel and ministers of Christ's redemptive work.

Here there is seen in all its grandeur the figure of the minister of the sacrament of penance, who by very ancient custom is called the confessor.

Just as at the altar where he celebrates the eucharist and just as in each one of the sacraments, so the priest, as the minister of penance, acts *"in persona Christi."* The Christ whom he makes present and who accomplishes the mystery of the forgiveness of sins is the Christ who appears as the brother of man,[163] the merciful high priest, faithful and compassionate,[164] the shepherd intent on finding the lost sheep,[165] the physician who heals and comforts,[166] the one master who teaches the truth and reveals the ways of God,[167] the judge of the living and the dead,[168] who judges according to the truth and not according to appearances.[169]

This is undoubtedly the most difficult and sensitive, the most exhausting and demanding ministry of the priest, but also one of the most beautiful and consoling. Precisely for this reason and with awareness also of the strong recommendation of the synod, I will never grow weary of exhorting my brothers, the bishops and priests, to the faithful and diligent performance of this ministry.[170] Before the consciences of the faithful, who open up to him with a mixture of fear and trust, the confessor is called to a lofty task which is one of service and penance and human reconciliation. It is a task of learning the weaknesses and falls of those faithful people, assessing their desire for renewal and their efforts to achieve it, discerning the action of the Holy Spirit in their hearts, imparting to them a forgiveness which God alone can grant, "celebrating" their reconciliation with the Father, portrayed in the parable of the prodigal son, reinstating these redeemed sinners in the ecclesial community with their brothers and sisters, and paternally admonishing these penitents with a firm, encouraging and friendly "Do not sin again."[171]

For the effective performance of this ministry, the confessor must necessarily have human qualities of prudence, discretion, discernment and a firmness tempered by gentleness and kindness. He must likewise have a serious and careful preparation, not fragmentary but complete and harmonious, in the different branches of theology, pedagogy and psychology, in the methodology of dialogue and above all in a living and communicable knowledge of the word of God. But it is even more necessary that he should live an intense and genuine spiritual life. In order to lead others along the path of Christian perfection the minister of penance himself must first travel this path. More by actions than by long speeches he must give proof of real experience of lived prayer, the practice of the theological and moral virtues of the Gospel, faithful obedience to the will of God, love of the church and docility to her magisterium.

All this fund of human gifts, Christian virtues and pastoral capabilities has to be worked for and is only acquired with effort. Every priest must be trained for the ministry of sacramental penance from his years in the seminary, not only through the study of dogmatic, moral, spiritual and pastoral theology (which are simply parts of a whole), but also through the study of the human sciences, training in dialogue and especially in how to deal with people in the pastoral context. He must then be guided and looked after in his first activities. He must always ensure his own improvement and updating by means of permanent study. What a wealth of grace, true life and spiritual radiation would be poured out on the church if every priest were careful never to miss through negligence or various excuses the appointment with the faithful in the confessional and if he were even more careful never to go to it unprepared or lacking the necessary human qualities and spiritual and pastoral preparation!

In this regard I cannot but recall with devout admiration those extraordinary apostles of the confessional such as St. John Nepomucene, St. John Vianney, St. Joseph Cafasso and St. Leo-pold of Castelnuovo, to mention only the best-known confessors whom the church has added to the list of her saints. But I also wish to pay homage to the innumerable host of holy and almost always anonymous confessors to whom is owed the salvation of so many souls who have been helped by them in conversion, in the struggle against sin and temptation, in spiritual progress and, in a word, in achieving holiness. I do not hesitate to say that even the great canonized saints are generally the fruit of those confessionals, and not only the saints but also the spiritual patrimony of the church and the flowering of a civilization permeated with the Christian spirit! Praise then to this silent army of our brothers who have served well and serve each day the cause of reconciliation through the ministry of sacramental penance!

The Sacrament of Forgiveness

30. From the revelation of the value of this ministry and power to forgive sins, conferred by Christ on the apostles and their successors, there developed in the church an awareness of the sign of forgiveness, conferred through the sacrament of penance. It is the certainty that the Lord Jesus himself instituted and entrusted to the church—as a gift of his goodness and loving kindness[172] to be offered to all—a special sacrament for the forgiveness of sins committed after baptism.

The practice of this sacrament, as regards its celebration and form, has undergone a long process of development as is attested to by the most ancient sacramentaries, the documents of councils and episcopal synods, the preaching of the fathers and the teaching of the doctors of the church. But with regard to the substance of the sacrament there has always remained firm and unchanged in the consciousness of the church the certainty that, by the will of Christ, forgiveness is offered to each individual by means of sacramental absolution given by the ministers of penance. It is a certainty reaffirmed with particular vigor both by the Council of Trent[173] and by the Second Vatican Council: "Those who approach the sacrament of penance obtain pardon from God's mercy for the offenses committed against him, and are, at the same time, reconciled with the church which they have wounded by their sins and which by charity, by example and by prayer works for their conversion."[174] And as an essential element of faith concerning the value and purpose of penance it must be reaffirmed that our savior Jesus Christ instituted in his church the sacrament of penance so that the faithful who have fallen into sin after baptism might receive grace and be reconciled with God.[175]

The church's faith in this sacrament involves certain other fundamental truths which cannot be disregarded. The sacramental rite of penance, in its evolution and variation of actual forms, has always preserved and highlighted these truths. When it recommended a reform of this rite, the Second Vatican Council intended to ensure that it would express these truths even more clearly,[176] and this has come about with the new Rite of Penance.[177] For the latter has made its own the whole of the teaching brought together by the Council of Trent, transferring it from its particular historical context (that of a resolute effort to clarify doctrine in the face of the serious deviations from the church's genuine teaching), in order to translate it faithfully into terms more in keeping with the context of our own time.

Some Fundamental Convictions

31. The truths mentioned above, powerfully and clearly confirmed by the synod and contained in the propositiones, can be summarized in the following convictions of faith, to which are connected all the other affirmations of the Catholic doctrine on the sacrament of penance.

I. The first conviction is that for a Christian the sacrament of penance is the ordinary way of obtaining forgiveness and the remission of serious sin committed after baptism. Certainly the Savior and his salvific action are not so bound to a sacramental sign as to be unable in any period or area of the history of salvation to work outside and above the sacraments. But in the school of faith we learn that the same Savior desired and provided that the simple and precious sacraments of faith would ordinarily be the effective means through which his redemptive power passes and operates. It would therefore be foolish, as well as presumptuous, to wish arbitrarily to disregard the means of grace and salvation which the Lord has provided and, in the specific case, to claim to receive forgiveness while doing without the sacrament which was instituted by Christ precisely for forgiveness. The renewal of the rites carried out after the council does not sanction any illusion or alteration in this direction.

According to the church's intention, it was and is meant to stir up in each one of us a new impulse toward the renewal of our interior attitude; toward a deeper understanding of the nature of the sacrament of penance; toward a reception of the sacrament which is more filled with faith, not anxious but trusting; toward a more frequent celebration of the sacrament which is seen to be completely filled with the Lord's merciful love.

II. The second conviction concerns the function of the sacrament of penance for those who have recourse to it. According to the most ancient traditional idea, the sacrament is a kind of judicial action; but this takes place before a tribunal of mercy rather than of strict and rigorous justice, which is comparable to human tribunals only by analogy,"[178] namely insofar as sinners reveal their sins and their condition as creatures subject to sin; they commit themselves to renouncing and combating sin; accept the punishment (sacramental penance) which the confessor imposes on them and receive absolution from him.

But as it reflects on the function of this sacrament, the church's consciousness discerns in it, over and above the character of judgment in the sense just mentioned, a healing of a medicinal character. And this is linked to the fact that the Gospel frequently presents Christ as healer,[179] while his redemptive work is often called, from Christian antiquity, *medicina salutis.* "I wish to heal, not accuse," St. Augustine said, referring to the exercise of the pastoral activity regarding penance,[180] and it is thanks to the medicine of confession that the experience of sin does not degenerate into despair.[181] The Rite of Penance alludes to this healing aspect of the sacrament,[182] to which modern man is perhaps more sensitive, seeing as he does in sin the element of error but even more the element of weakness and human frailty.

Whether as a tribunal of mercy or a place of spiritual healing, under both aspects the sacrament requires a knowledge of the sinner's heart in order to be able to judge and absolve, to cure and heal. Precisely for this reason the sacrament involves on the part of the penitent a sincere and complete confession of sins. This therefore has a *raison d'etre* not only inspired by ascetical purposes (as an exercise of humility and mortification), but one that is inherent in the very nature of the sacrament.

III. The third conviction, which is one that I wish to emphasize, concerns the realities or parts which make up the sacramental sign of forgiveness and reconciliation. Some of these realities are acts of the penitent, of varying importance but each indispensable either for the validity, the completeness or the fruitfulness of the sign.

First of all, an indispensable condition is the rectitude and clarity of the penitent's conscience. People cannot come to true and genuine repentance until they realize that sin is contrary to the ethical norm written in their inmost being;[183] until they admit that they have had a personal and responsible experience of this contrast; until they say not only that "sin exists" but also "I have sinned"; until they admit that sin has introduced a division into their consciences which then pervades their whole being and separates them from God and from their brothers and sisters. The sacramental sign of this clarity of conscience is the act traditionally called the examination of conscience, an act that must never be one of anxious psychological introspection, but a sincere and calm comparison with the interior moral law, with the evangelical norms proposed by the church, with Jesus Christ himself, who is our teacher and model of life, and with the heavenly Father, who calls us to goodness and perfection.[184]

But the essential act of penance, on the part of the penitent, is contrition, a clear and decisive rejection of the sin committed, together with a resolution not to commit it again,[185] out of the love which one has for God and which is reborn with repentance. Understood in this way, contrition is therefore the beginning and the heart of conversion, of that evangelical *metanoia* which brings the person back to God like the prodigal son returning to his father, and which has in the sacrament of penance its visible sign and which perfects attrition. Hence "upon this contrition of heart depends the truth of penance."[186]

While reiterating everything that the church, inspired by God's word, teaches about contrition, I particularly wish to emphasize here just one aspect of this doctrine. It is one that should be better known and considered. Conversion and contrition are often considered under the aspect of the undeniable demands which they involve and under the aspect of the mortification which they impose for the purpose of bringing about a radical change of life. But we all do well to recall and emphasize the fact that contrition and conversion are even more a drawing near to the holiness of God, a rediscovery of one's true identity, which has been upset and disturbed by sin, a liberation in the very depth of self and thus a regaining of lost joy, the joy of being saved,[187] which the majority of people in our time are no longer capable of experiencing.

We therefore understand why, from the earliest Christian times, in line with the apostles and with Christ, the church has included in the sacramental sign of penance the confession of sins. This latter takes on such importance that for centuries the usual name of the sacrament has been and still is that of confession. The confession of sins is required, first of all, because the sinner must be known by the person who in the sacrament exercises the role of judge. He has to evaluate both the seriousness of the sins and the repentance of the penitent; he also exercises the role of the healer and must acquaint himself with the condition of the sick person in order to treat and heal him. But the individual confession also has the value of a sign: a sign of the meeting of the sinner with the mediation of the church in the person of the minister; a sign of the person's revealing of self as a sinner in the sight of God and the church, of facing his own sinful condition in the eyes of God. The confession of sins therefore cannot be reduced to a mere attempt at psychological self-liberation even though it corresponds to that legitimate and natural need, inherent in the human heart, to open oneself to another. It is a liturgical act, solemn in its dramatic nature, yet humble and sober in the grandeur of its meaning. It is the act of the prodigal son who returns to his Father and is welcomed by him with the kiss of peace. It is an act of honesty and courage. It is an act of entrusting oneself, beyond sin, to the mercy that forgives.[188] Thus we understand why the confession of sins must ordinarily be individual not collective, just as sin is a deeply personal matter. But at the same time this confession in a way forces sin out of the secret of the heart and thus out of the area of pure individuality, emphasizing its social character as well, for through the minister of penance it is the ecclesial community, which has been wounded by sin, that welcomes anew the repentant and forgiven sinner.

The other essential stage of the sacrament of penance this time belongs to the confessor as judge and healer, a figure of God the Father welcoming and forgiving the one who returns: This is the absolution. The words which express it and the gestures that accompany it in the old and in the new Rite of Penance are significantly simple in their grandeur. The sacramental formula "I absolve you" and the imposition of the hand and the Sign of the Cross made over the penitent show that at this moment the contrite and converted sinner comes into contact with the power and mercy of God. It is the moment at which, in response to the penitent, the Trinity becomes present in order to blot out sin and restore innocence. And the saving power of the passion, death and resurrection of Jesus is also imparted to the penitent as the "mercy stronger than sin and offense," as I defined it in my encyclical *Dives in Misericordia.* God is always the one who is principally offended by sin—*"Tibi soli peccavi!"*—and God alone can forgive. Hence the absolution that the priest, the minister of forgiveness, though himself a sinner, grants to the penitent is the effective sign of the intervention of the Father in every absolution and the sign of the "resurrection" from "spiritual death" which is renewed each time that the sacrament of penance is administered. Only faith can give us certainty that at that moment every sin is forgiven and blotted out by the mysterious intervention of the Savior.

Satisfaction is the final act which crowns the sacramental sign of penance. In some countries the act which the forgiven and absolved penitent agrees to perform after receiving absolution is called precisely the penance. What is the meaning of this satisfaction that one makes or the penance that one performs? Certainly it is not a price that one pays for the sin absolved and for the forgiveness obtained: No human price can match what is obtained, which is the fruit of Christ's precious blood. Acts of satisfaction—which, while remaining simple and humble, should be made to express more clearly all that they signify—mean a number of valuable things: They are the sign of the personal commitment that the Christian has made to God in the sacrament to begin a new life (and therefore they should not be reduced to mere formulas to be recited, but should consist of acts of worship, charity, mercy or reparation). They include the idea that the pardoned sinner is able to join his own physical and spiritual mortification—which has been sought after or at least accepted—to the passion of Jesus, who has obtained the forgiveness for him. They remind us that even after absolution there remains in the Christian a dark area due to the wound of sin, to the imperfection of love in repentance, to the weakening of the spiritual faculties. It is an area in which there still operates an infectious source of sin which must always be fought with mortification and penance. This is the meaning of the humble but sincere act of satisfaction.[189]

IV. There remains to be made a brief mention of other important convictions about the sacrament of penance.

First of all, it must be emphasized that nothing is more personal and intimate that this sacrament, in which the sinner stands alone before God with his sin, repentance and trust. No one can repent in his place or ask forgiveness in his name. There is a certain solitude of the sinner in his sin, and this can be seen dramatically represented in Cain with sin "crouching at his door," as the Book of Genesis says so effectively, and with the distinctive mark on his forehead;[190] in David, admonished by the prophet Nathan;[191] or in the prodigal son when he realizes the condition to which he has reduced himself by staying away from his father and decides to return to him.[192] Everything takes place between the individual alone and God. But at the same time one cannot deny the social nature of this sacrament, in which the whole church—militant, suffering and glorious in heaven—comes to the aid of the penitent and welcomes him again into her bosom, especially as it was the whole church which had been offended and wounded by his sin. As the minister of penance, the priest by virtue of his sacred office appears as the witness and representative of this ecclesial nature of the sacrament. The individual nature and ecclesial nature are two complementary aspects of the sacrament which the progressive reform of the Rite of Penance, especially that contained in the *Ordo Paenitentiae* promulgated by Paul VI, has sought to emphasize and to make more meaningful in its celebration.

V. Second, it must be emphasized that the most precious result of the forgiveness obtained in the sacrament of penance consists in reconciliation with God, which takes place in the inmost heart of the son who was lost and found again, which every penitent is. But it has to be added that this reconciliation with God leads, as it were, to other reconciliations which repair the breaches caused by sin. The forgiven penitent is reconciled with himself in his inmost being, where he regains his own true identity. He is reconciled with his brethren whom he has in some way attacked and wounded. He is reconciled with the church. He is reconciled with all creation.

As a result of an awareness of this, at the end of the celebration there arises in the penitent a sense of gratitude to God for the gift of divine mercy received, and the church invites the penitent to have this sense of gratitude.

Every confessional is a special and blessed place from which, with divisions wiped away, there is born new and uncontaminated a reconciled individual—a reconciled world!

VI. Last, I particularly wish to speak of one final consideration, one which concerns all of us priests, who are the ministers of the sacrament of penance.[193] The priest's celebration of the eucharist and administration of the other sacraments, his pastoral zeal, his relationship with the faithful, his communion with his brother priests, his collaboration with his bishop, his life of prayer—in a word, the whole of his priestly existence, suffers an inexorable decline if by negligence or for some other reason he fails to receive the sacrament of penance at regular intervals and in a spirit of genuine faith and devotion. If a priest were no longer to go to confession or properly confess his sins, his priestly being and his priestly action would feel its effects very soon and this would also be noticed by the community of which he was the pastor.

But I also add that even in order to be a good and effective minister of penance the priest needs to have recourse to the source of grace and holiness present in this sacrament. We priests, on the basis of our personal experience, can certainly say that the more careful we are to receive the sacrament of penance and to approach it frequently and with good dispositions, the better we fulfill our own ministry as confessors and ensure that our penitents benefit from it. And on the other hand, this ministry would lose much of its effectiveness if in some way we were to stop being good penitents. Such is the internal logic of this great sacrament. It invites all of us priests of Christ to pay renewed attention to our personal confession.

Personal experience in its turn becomes and must become today an incentive for the diligent, regular, patient and fervent exercise of the sacred ministry of penance, to which we are committed by the very fact of our priesthood and our vocation as pastors and servants of our brothers and sisters. Also with this present exhortation I therefore address an earnest invitation to all the priests of the world, especially to my brothers in the episcopacy and to pastors of souls, an invitation to make every effort to encourage the faithful to make use of this sacrament. I urge them to use all possible and suitable means to ensure that the greatest possible number of our brothers and sisters receive the "grace that has been given to us" through penance for the reconciliation of every soul and of the whole world with God in Christ.

Forms of Celebration

32. Following the suggestions of the Second Vatican Council, the *Ordo Paenitentiae* provided three rites which, while always keeping intact the essential elements, make it possible to adapt the celebration of the sacrament of penance to particular pastoral circumstances.

The first form—reconciliation of individual penitents—is the only normal and ordinary way of celebrating the sacrament, and it cannot and must not be allowed to fall into disuse or be neglected. The second form—reconciliation of a number of penitents with individual confession and absolution—even though in the preparatory acts it helps to give greater emphasis to the community aspects of the sacrament, is the same as the first form in the culminating sacramental act, namely individual confession and individual absolution of sins. It can thus be regarded as equal to the first form as regards the normality of the rite. The third form however—reconciliation of a number of penitents with general confession and absolution—is exceptional in character. It is therefore not left to free choice but is regulated by a special discipline.

The first form makes possible a highlighting of the more personal—and essential—aspects which are included in the penitential process. The dialogue between penitent and confessor, the sum of the elements used (the biblical texts, the choice of the forms of "satisfaction," etc.), make the sacramental celebration correspond more closely to the concrete situation of the penitent. The value of these elements are perceived when one considers the different reasons that bring a Christian to sacramental penance: a need for personal reconciliation and readmission to friendship with God by regaining the grace lost by sin; a need to check one's spiritual progress and sometimes a need for a more accurate discernment of one's vocation; on many other occasions a need and a desire to escape from a state of spiritual apathy and religious crisis. Thanks then to its individual character, the first form of celebration makes it possible to link the sacrament of penance with something which is different but readily linked with it: I am referring to spiritual direction. So it is certainly true that personal decision and commitment are clearly signified and promoted in this first form.

The second form of celebration, precisely by its specific dimension, highlights certain aspects of great importance: The word of God listened to in common has a remarkable effect as compared to its individual reading and better emphasizes the ecclesial character of conversion and reconciliation. It is particularly meaningful at various seasons of the liturgical year and in connection with events of special pastoral importance. The only point that needs mentioning here is that for celebrating the second form there should be an adequate number of confessors present.

It is therefore natural that the criteria for deciding which of the two forms of celebration to use should be dictated not by situational and subjective reasons, but by a desire to secure the true spiritual good of the faithful in obedience to the penitential discipline of the church.

We shall also do well to recall that, for a balanced spiritual and pastoral orientation in this regard, great importance must continue to be given to teaching the faithful also to make use of the sacrament of penance for venial sins alone, as is borne out by a centuries-old doctrinal tradition and practice.

Though the church knows and teaches that venial sins are forgiven in other ways too—for instance, by acts of sorrow, works of charity, prayer, penitential rites—she does not cease to remind everyone of the special usefulness of the sacramental moment for these sins too. The frequent use of the sacrament— to which some categories of the faithful are in fact held— strengthens the awareness that even minor sins offend God and harm the church, the body of Christ. Its celebration then becomes for the faithful "the occasion and the incentive to conform themselves more closely to Christ and to make themselves more docile to the voice of the Spirit."[194] Above all it should be emphasized that the grace proper to the sacramental celebration has a great remedial power and helps to remove the very roots of sin.

Attention to the actual celebration,[195] with special reference to the importance of the word of God which is read, recalled and explained, when this is possible and suitable, to the faithful and with them, will help to give fresh life to the practice of the sacrament and prevent it from declining into a mere formality and routine. The penitent will be helped rather to discover that he or she is living a salvific event capable of inspiring fresh life and giving true peace of heart. This careful attention to the celebration will also lead the individual churches to arrange special times for the celebration of the sacrament. It will also be an incentive to teaching the faithful, especially children and young people, to accustom themselves to keeping to these times except in cases of necessity, when the parish priest must always show a ready willingness to receive whoever comes to him.

Celebration of the Sacrament with General Absolution

33. The new liturgical regulation and, more recently, the Code of Canon Law,[196] specify the conditions which make it lawful to use "the rite of reconciliation of a number of penitents with general confession and absolution." The norms and regulations given on this point, which are the result of mature and balanced consideration, must be accepted and applied in such a way as to avoid any sort of arbitrary interpretation.

It is opportune to reflect more deeply on the reasons which order the celebration of penance in one of the first two forms and permit the use of the third form. First of all, there is the reason of fidelity to the will of the Lord Jesus, transmitted by the doctrine of the church, and also the reason of obedience to the church's laws. The synod repeated in one of its *propositiones* the unchanged teaching which the church has derived from the most ancient tradition, and it repeated the law with which she has codified the ancient penitential practice: The individual and integral confession of sins with individual absolution constitutes the only ordinary way in which the faithful who are conscious of serious sin are reconciled with God and with the church. From this confirmation of the church's teaching it is clear that every serious sin must always be stated, with its determining circumstances, in an individual confession.

Then there is a reason of the pastoral order. While it is true that, when the conditions required by canonical discipline occur, use may be made of the third form of celebration, it must not be forgotten that this form cannot become an ordinary one, and it cannot and must not be used—as the synod repeated—except "in cases of grave necessity." And there remains unchanged the obligation to make an individual confession of serious sins before again having recourse to another general absolution. The bishop therefore, who is the only one competent in his own diocese to assess whether the conditions actually exist which canon law lays down for the use of the third form, will give this judgment with a grave obligation on his own conscience, with full respect for the law and practice of the church and also taking into account the criteria and guidelines agreed upon—on the basis of the doctrinal and pastoral considerations explained above—with the other members of the episcopal conference. Equally it will always be a matter of genuine pastoral concern to lay down and guarantee the conditions that make recourse to the third form capable of producing the spiritual fruits for which it is meant. The exceptional use of the third form of celebration must never lead to a lesser regard for, still less an abandonment of, the ordinary forms nor must it lead to this form being considered an alternative to the other two forms. It is not in fact left to the freedom of pastors and the faithful to choose from among these forms the one considered most suitable. It remains the obligation of pastors to facilitate for the faithful the practice of integral and individual confession of sins, which constitutes for them not only a duty but also an inviolable and inalienable right, besides being something needed by the soul. For the faithful, the use of the third form of celebration involves the obligation of following all the norms regulating its exercise, including that of not having recourse again to general absolution before a normal integral and individual confession of sins, which must be made as soon as possible. Before granting absolution the priest must inform and instruct the faithful about this norm and about the obligation to observe it.

With this reminder of the doctrine and the law of the church I wish to instill into everyone the lively sense of responsibility which must guide us when we deal with sacred things like the sacraments, which are not our property, or like consciences, which have a right not to be left in uncertainty and confusion. The sacraments and consciences, I repeat, are sacred, and both require that we serve them in truth.

This is the reason for the church's law.

Some More Delicate Cases

34. I consider it my duty to mention at this point, if very briefly, a pastoral case that the synod dealt with—insofar as it was able to do so—and which it also considered in one of the *propositiones.* I am referring to certain situations, not infrequent today, affecting Christians who wish to continue their sacramental religious practice, but who are prevented from doing so by their personal condition, which is not in harmony with the commitments freely undertaken before God and the church. These are situations which seem particularly delicate and almost inextricable.

Numerous interventions during the synod, expressing the general thought of the fathers, emphasized the coexistence and mutual influence of two equally important principles in relation to these cases. The first principle is that of compassion and mercy, whereby the church, as the continuer in history of Christ's presence and work, not wishing the death of the sinner but that the sinner should be converted and live,[197] and careful not to break the bruised reed or to quench the dimly burning wick,[198] ever seeks to offer, as far as possible, the path of return to God and of reconciliation with him. The other principle is that of truth and consistency, whereby the church does not agree to call good evil and evil good. Basing herself on these two complementary principles, the church can only invite her children who find themselves in these painful situations to approach the divine mercy by other ways, not however through the sacraments of penance and the eucharist until such time as they have attained the required dispositions.

On this matter, which also deeply torments our pastoral hearts, it seemed my precise duty to say clear words in the apostolic exhortation *Familiaris Consortio,* as regards the case of the divorced and remarried,[199] and likewise the case of Christians living together in an irregular union.

At the same time and together with the synod, I feel that it is my clear duty to urge the ecclesial communities and especially the bishops to provide all possible assistance to those priests who have fallen short of the grave commitments which they undertook at their ordination and who are living in irregular situations. None of these brothers of ours should feel abandoned by the church.

For all those who are not at the present moment in the objective conditions required by the sacrament of penance, the church's manifestations of maternal kindness, the support of acts of piety apart from sacramental ones, a sincere effort to maintain contact with the Lord, attendance at Mass and the frequent repetition of acts of faith, hope, charity and sorrow made as perfectly as possible can prepare the way for full reconciliation at the hour that providence alone knows.

Concluding Expression of Hope

35. At the end of this document I hear echoing within me and I desire to repeat to all of you the exhortation which the first bishop of Rome, at a critical hour of the beginning of the church, addressed "to the exiles of the dispersion...chosen and destined by God the Father...: Have unity of spirit, sympathy, love of the brethren, a tender heart and a humble mind."[200] The apostle urged: "Have unity of spirit." But he immediately went on to point out the sins against harmony and peace which must be avoided: "Do not return evil for evil or reviling for reviling; but on the contrary bless, for to this you have been called, that you may obtain a blessing." And he ended with a word of encouragement and hope: "Who is there to harm you if you are zealous for what is right?"[201]

At an hour of history which is no less critical, I dare to join my exhortation to that of the prince of the apostles, the first to occupy this See of Rome as a witness to Christ and as pastor of the church, and who here "presided in charity" before the entire world. In communion with the bishops who are the successors of the apostles and supported by the collegial reflection that many of them, meeting in the synod, devoted to the topics and problems of reconciliation, I too wish to speak to you with the same spirit of the fisherman of Galilee when he said to our brothers and sisters in the faith, distant in time but so closely linked in heart: "Have unity of spirit.... Do not return evil for evil.... Be zealous for what is right."[202] And he added: "It is better to suffer for doing right, if that should be God's will, than for doing wrong."[203]

This exhortation is completely permeated by words which Peter had heard from Jesus himself and by ideas which formed part of his "good news": the new commandment of love of neighbor; the yearning for and commitment to unity; the beatitudes of mercy and patience in persecution for the sake of justice; the repaying of evil with good; the forgiveness of offenses; the love of enemies. In these words and ideas is the original and transcendent synthesis of the Christian ethic or, more accurately and more profoundly, of the spirituality of the new covenant in Jesus Christ.

I entrust to the Father, rich in mercy, I entrust to the Son of God, made man as our redeemer and reconciler, I entrust to the Holy Spirit, source of unity and peace, this call of mine, as father and pastor, to penance and reconciliation. May the most holy and adorable Trinity cause to spring up in the church and in the world the small seed which at this hour I plant in the generous soil of many human hearts.

In order that in the not too distant future abundant fruits may come from it, I invite you all to join me in turning to Christ's heart, the eloquent sign of the divine mercy, the "propitiation for our sins," "our peace and reconciliation,"[204] that we may draw from it an interior encouragement to hate sin and to be converted to God, and find in it the divine kindness which lovingly responds to human repentance.

I likewise invite you to turn with me to the immaculate heart of Mary, mother of Jesus, in whom "is effected the reconciliation of God with humanity..., is accomplished the work of reconciliation, because she has received from God the fullness of grace in virtue of the redemptive sacrifice of Christ."[205] Truly Mary has been associated with God, by virtue of her divine motherhood, in the work of reconciliation.[206]

Into the hands of this mother, whose fiat marked the beginning of that "fullness of time" in which Christ accomplished the reconciliation of humanity with God, to her immaculate heart—to which we have repeatedly entrusted the whole of humanity, disturbed by sin and tormented by so many tensions and conflicts—I now in a special way entrust this intention: that through her intercession humanity may discover and travel the path of penance, the only path that can lead it to full reconciliation.

To all of you who in a spirit of ecclesial communion in obedience and faith[207] receive the indications, suggestions and directives contained in this document and seek to put them into living pastoral practice, I willingly impart my apostolic blessing.

Given in Rome at St. Peter's on December 2, the first Sunday of Advent, in the year 1984, the seventh of my pontificate.

Joannes Paulus PP. II

Notes

1. Mk 1:15.

2. Cf Pope John Paul II, opening speech at the Third General Conference of the Latin American Episcopate: *AAS* 71 (1979), 198-204.

3. The idea of a "shattered world" is seen in the works of numerous contemporary writers, both Christian and non-Christian, witnesses of man's condition in this tormented period of history.

4. Cf Pastoral Constitution on the Church in the Modern World *Gaudium et Spes*, 3, 43 and 44; Decree on the Ministry and Life of Priests *Presbyterorum Ordinis*, 12; Pope Paul VI, encyclical *Ecclesiam Suam: AAS* 56 (1964), 609-659.

5. At the very beginning of the church, the apostle Paul wrote with words of fire about division in the body of the church, in the famous passage 1 Cor 1:10-16. Years later, St. Clement of Rome was also to write to the Corinthians, to condemn the wounds inside that community: cf Letter to the Corinthians, III-VI; LVII: *Patres Apostolici,* ed. Funk, I, 103-109; 171-173. We know that from the earliest fathers onward Christ's seamless robe, which the soldiers did not divide, became an image of the church's unity: cf St. Cyprian, *De Ecclesiae Catholicae Unitate*, 7: CCL 3/1, 254f; St. Augustine, *In Ioannis Evangelium Tractatus,* 118, 4: CCL 36, 656f; St. Bede the Venerable, *In Marci Evangelium Expositio,* IV, 15: CCL 120, 630; *In Lucae Evangelium Expositio,* VI, 23: CCL 120, 403; *In S. Ioannis Evangelium Expositio,* 19: PL 92, 911f.

6. The encyclical *Pacem in Terris,* John XXIII's spiritual testament, is often considered a "social document" and even a "political message," and in fact it is if these terms are understood in their broadest sense. As is evident more than twenty years after its publication, the document is in fact more than a strategy for the peaceful coexistence of people and nations; it is a pressing reminder of the higher values without which peace on earth becomes a mere dream. One of these values is precisely that of reconciliation among people, and John XXIII often referred to this subject. With regard to Paul VI, it will suffice to recall that in calling the church and the world to celebrate the Holy Year of 1975, he wished "renewal and reconciliation" to be the central idea of that important event. Nor can one

forget the catechesis which he devoted to this key theme, also in explaining the jubilee itself.

7. As I wrote in the bull of indiction of the Jubilee Year of the Redemption: "This special time, when all Christians are called upon to realize more profoundly their vocation to reconciliation with the Father in the Son, will only reach its full achievement if it leads to a fresh commitment by each and every person to the service of reconciliation, not only among all the disciples of Christ but also among all men and women": bull *Aperite Portas Redemptori*, 3: *AAS* 75 (1983), 93.

8. The theme of the synod was, more precisely, "Reconciliation and Penance in the Mission of the Church."

9. Cf Mt 4:17; Mk 1:15.

10. Cf Lk 3:8.

11. Cf Mt 16:24-26; Mk 8:34-36; Lk 9:23-25.

12. Eph 4:23f.

13. Cf 1 Cor 3:1-20.

14. Cf Col 3:1f.

15. "We beseech you on behalf of Christ, be reconciled to God": 2 Cor 5:20.

16. "We also rejoice in God through our Lord Jesus Christ, through whom we have now received our reconciliation": Rom 5:11; cf Col 1:20.

17. The Second Vatican Council noted: "The dichotomy affecting the modern world is, in fact, a symptom of the deeper dichotomy that is in man himself. He is the meeting point of many conflicting forces. In his condition as a created being he is subject to a thousand shortcomings, but feels untrammeled in his inclinations and destined for a higher form of life. Torn by a welter of anxieties he is compelled to choose between them and repudiate some among them. Worse still, feeble and sinful as he is, he often does the very thing he hates and does not do what he wants (cf Rom 7:14ff). And so he feels himself divided, and the result is a host of discords in social life." *Gaudium et Spes*, 10.

18. Cf Col 1:19f.

19. Cf Pope John Paul II, encyclical *Dives in Misericordia*, 5-6: *AAS* 72 (1980), 1193-1199.

20. Cf Lk 15:11-32.

21. In the Old Testament, the Book of Jonah is a wonderful anticipation and figure of this aspect of the parable. Jonah's sin is that he was "displeased...exceedingly and he was angry" because God is "a gracious God and merciful, slow to anger, and abounding in steadfast love, and repentest of evil." His sin is also that of pitying a castor oil plant "which came into being in a night, and perished in a night" and not understanding that the Lord pities Niniveh: cf Jon 4.

22. Cf Rom 5:10f.; cf Col 1:20-22.

23. Cf 2 Cor 5:18, 20.

24. Jn 11:52.

25. Cf Col 1:20.

26. Cf Sir 44:17.

27. Eph 2:14.

28. Eucharistic Prayer 3.

29. Cf Mt 5:23f.

30. Ibid., 27:46; Mk 15:34, Ps 22(21):2.

31. Cf Eph 2:14-16.

32. St. Leo the Great, *Tractatus* 63 (*De Passione Domini*, 12), 6: CCL 138/A, 386.

33. Cf 2 Cor 5:18f.

34. Dogmatic Constitution on the Church *Lumen Gentium*, 1.

35. "The church is also by her nature always reconciling, handing on to others the gift that she herself has received, the gift of having been forgiven and made one with God": Pope John Paul II, Homily at Liverpool, May 30, 1982: *Insegnamenti*, V, 2 (1982), 1992.

36. Cf Acts 15:2-33.

37. Cf Apostolic exhortation *Evangelii Nuntiandi*, 13: *AAS* 68 (1976), 12f.

38. Cf Pope John Paul II, apostolic exhortation *Catechesi Tradendae, 24: AAS* 71 (1979), 1297.

39. Cf Pope Paul VI, encyclical, *Ecclesiam Suam: ASS* 56 (1964), 609-659.

40. Cf 2 Cor 5:20.

41. Cf 1 Jn 4:8.

42. Cf Wis 11:23-26; Gn 1:27; Ps 8:4-8.

43. Cf Wis 2:24.

44. Cf Gn 3:12f; 4:1-16.

45. Cf Eph 2:4.

46. Cf ibid., 1:10.

47. Jn 13:34.

48. Cf Second Vatican Council, Pastoral Constitution on the Church in the Modern World *Gaudium et Spes*, 38.

49. Cf Mk 1:15.

50. Cf 2 Cor 5:20.

51. Cf Eph 2:14-16.

52. Cf St. Augustine, *De Civitate Dei*, XXII, 17: CCL 48, 835f; St. Thomas Aquinas, *Summa Theologiae*, III pars, q. 64, art. 2 *ad tertium*.

53. Cf Pope Paul VI, Allocution at the Closing of the Third Session of the Second Vatican Ecumenical Council, November 21, 1964: *ASS* 56 (1964), 1015-1018.

54. Second Vatican Council, Dogmatic Constitution on the Church *Lumen Gentium*, 39.

55. Ibid., Decree on Ecumenism *Unitatis Redintegratio*, 4.

56. 1 Jn 1:8-9.

57. 1 Jn 3:20; cf my reference to this passage in my address at the general audience of March 14, 1984: *Insegnamenti*, VII, 1 (1984) 683.

58. Cf 2 Sm 11-12.

59. Cf Ps 50(51):3-4.

60. Cf Lk 15:18, 21.

61. *Lettere*, Florence 1970, I, pp. 3f; *Il Dialogo della Divina Providenza*, Rome 1980, *passim*.

62. Cf Rom 3:23-26.

63. Cf Eph 1:18.

64. Cf Gn 11:1-9.

65. Cf Ps 127 (126):1.

66. Cf 2 Thes 2:7.

67. Cf Rom 7:7-25; Eph 2:2; 6:12.

68. The terminology used in the Septuagint Greek translation and in the New Testament for sin is significant. The most common term for sin is *hamartia*, with its various derivatives. It expresses the concept of offending more or less gravely against a norm or law, or against a person or even a divinity. But sin is also called *adikia*, and the concept here is of acting unjustly. The Bible also speaks of *parabasis* (transgression), *asebeia* (impiety) and other concepts. They all convey the image of sin.

69. Gn 3:5: "And you will be like God, knowing good and evil"; cf also v. 22.

70. Cf ibid., 3:12.

71. Cf ibid., 4:2-16.

72. The expression from the French writer Elizabeth Leseur, *Journal et Pensees* de *Chaque Jour*, Paris 1918, p. 31.

73. Cf Mt 22:39; Mk 12:31; Lk 10:27f.

74. Cf Sacred Congregation for the Doctrine of the Faith: Instruction on Certain Aspects of the Theology of Liberation *Libertatis Nuntius*; August 6, 1984, IV, 14-15: *ASS* 76 (1984), 885f.

75. Cf Nm 15:30.

76. Cf Lv 18:26-30.

77. Cf ibid., 19:4.

78. Cf ibid., 20:1-7.

79. Cf Ex 21:17.

80. Cf Lv 4:2ff; 5:1ff; Nm 15:22-29.

81. Cf Mt 5:28; 6:23; 12:31f; 15:19; Mk 3:28-30; Rom 1:29-31; 13:13; Jas 4.

82. Cf Mt 5:17; 15:1-10; Mk 10:19; Lk 18:20.

83. Cf 1 Jn 5:16f.

84. Cf 1 Jn 17:3.

85. Cf 1 Jn 2:22.

86. Cf 1 Jn 5:21.

87. Cf 1 Jn 5:16-21.

88. Cf Mt 12:31f.

89. Cf St. Thomas Aquinas, *Summa Theologiae* II-II, q. 14, aa. 1-3.

90. Cf 1 Jn 3:20.

91. St. Thomas Aquinas, *Summa Theologiae*, II-II, q. 14, a. 3, *ad primum*.

92. Cf Phil 2:12.

93. Cf St. Augustine, *De Spiritu et Littera*, XXVIII: CSEL 60, 202f; *Enarrat. in ps.* 39, 22: CCL 38, 441; *Enchiridion ad Laurentium de Fide et Spe et Caritate*, XIX, 71: CCL 46, 88; *In Ioannis Evangelium Tractatus*, 12, 3, 14: CCL 36, 129.

94. St. Thomas Aquinas, *Summa Theologiae*, I-II, q. 72, a. 5.

95. Cf Council of Trent, Session VI, *De Iustificatione*, Chap. 2 and Canons 23, 25, 27: *Conciliorum Oecumenicorum Decreta*, Bologna 1973, 671 and 680f (DS 1573, 1575, 1577).

96. Cf Council of Trent, Session IV *De Iustificatione*, Chapt. 15: *Conciliorum Oecumenicorum Decreta*, ed. cit. 677 (DS 1544).

97. Pope John Paul II, Angelus Message of March 14, 1982: *Insegnamenti* V, 1 (1982), 861.

98. *Gaudium et Spes*, 16.

99. Pope John Paul II, Angelus Message of March 14, 1982: *Insegnamenti* V, 1 (1982), 860.

100. Pope Pius XII, Radio Message to the U.S. National Catechetical Congress in Boston (October 26, 1946): *Discorsi e Radiomessaggi*, VIII (1946), 288.

101. Cf Pope John Paul II, encyclical *Redemptor Hominis*, 15: *AAS* 71 (1979), 286-289.

102. Cf *Gaudium et Spes*, 3; cf 1 Jn 3:9.

103. Pope John Paul II, Address to the Bishops of the Eastern Region of France (April 1, 1982), 2: *Insegnamenti* V, 1 (1982), 1081.

104. 1 Tm 3:15f.

105. The text presents a certain difficulty, since the relative pronoun which opens the literal translation does not agree with the neuter *mysterion*. Some late manuscripts have adjusted the text in order to correct the grammar. But it was Paul's intention merely to put next to what he had written a venerable text which for him was fully explanatory.

106. The early Christian community expresses its faith in the crucified and glorified Christ, whom the angels adore and who is the Lord. But the striking element of this message remains the phrase "manifested in the flesh": that the eternal Son of God became man is the "great mystery."

107. 1 Jn 5:18f.

108. Ibid., 3:9.

109. 1 Tm 3:15.

110. 1 Jn 1:8.

111. Ibid., 5:19.

112. Cf Ps. 51(50):5.

113. Cf Eph. 2:4.

114. Cf Pope John Paul II, *Dives in Misericordia*, 8; 15: *AAS* 72 (1980), 1203-1207; 1231.

115. 2 Sm 12:13.

116. Ps 51(50):3.

117. Ibid., 51(50):7.

118. 2 Sm 12:13.

119. Cf 2 Cor 5:18.

120. Cf 2 Cor 5:19.

121. *Gaudium et Spes*, 92.

122. Decree on the Pastoral Office of Bishops in the Church *Christus Dominus*, 13; cf Declaration on Christian Education *Gravissimum Educationis*, 8; Decree on the Church's Missionary Activity *Ad Gentes*, 11-12.

123. Cf Pope Paul VI, Ecclesiam Suam, III: *AAS* 56 (1964), 639-659.

124. *Lumen Gentium*, 1, 9, 13.

125. Pope Paul VI, apostolic exhortation *Paterna Cum Benevolentia*: *AAS* 67 (1975), 5-23.

126. Cf *Unitatis Redintegratio*, 7-8.

127. Ibid., 4.

128. St. Augustine, *Sermo* 96, 7: *PL* 38, 588.

129. Pope John Paul II, Speech to Members of the Diplomatic Corps Accredited to the Holy See (January 15, 1983), 4, 6, 1 1: *AAS* 75 (1983), 376, 378f, 381.

130. Pope John Paul II, Homily at the Mass for the 16th World Day of Peace (January 1, 1983), 6: *Insegnamenti* VI, 1 (1983), 7.

131. Pope Paul VI, apostolic exhortation *Evangelii Nuntiandi*, 70: *AAS* 68 (1976), 59f.

132. 1 Tm 3:15.

133. Cf Mt 5:23f.

134. Cf ibid., 5:38-40.

135. Cf ibid., 6:12.

136. Cf ibid., 5:43ff.

137. Cf ibid., 18:21f.

138. Cf Mk 1:14; Mt 3:2; 4:17; Lk 3:8.

139. Cf Lk 15:17.

140. Ibid., 17:3f.

141. Cf Mt 3:2; Mk 1:2-6; Lk 3:1-6.

142. Cf *Gaudium et Spes*, 8, 16, 19, 26, 41,48.

143. Cf Declaration on Religious Liberty *Dignitatis Humanae*, 2, 3, 4.

144. Cf among many others the addresses at the general audiences of March 28, 1973: *Insegnamenti* XI (1973), 294ff; August 8, 1973: ibid., 772ff; November 7, 1973: ibid., 1054ff; March 13, 1974: *Insegnamenti* XII (1974), 230ff; May 8, 1974: ibid., 402ff; February 12, 1975: *Insegnamenti* XIII (1975), ibid., 290ff; July 13, 1977: *Insegnamenti* XV (1977), 710ff.

145. Cf Pope John Paul II, Angelus Message of March 17, 1982: *Insegnamenti* V, 1 (1982), 860f.

146. Cf Pope John Paul II, General Audience Address of August 17, 1983, 1-3: *Insegnamenti* VI, 2 (1983), 256f.

147. Heb 4:15.

148. Cf Mt 4:1-11; Mk 1:12f; Lk 4:1-13.

149. Cf 1 Cor 10:13.

150. Cf Mt 6:13; Lk 11:4.

151. 1 Pt 3:21.

152. Cf Rom 6:3f; Col 2:12.

153. Cf Mt 3:11; Lk 3:16; Jn 1:33; Acts 1:5; 11:16.

154. Cf Mt 3:15.

155. St. Augustine, *In Ioannis Evangelium Tractatus*, 26, 13: CCL 36, 266.

156. Sacred Congregation of Rites, Instruction on the Worship of the Eucharistic Mystery *Eucharisticum Mysterium* (May 25, 1967) 35: *AAS* 59 (1967), 560f.

157. Ps 78(77):38f.

158. Cf Jn 1:29; Is 53:7-12.

159. Cf Jn 5:27.

160. Cf Mt 9:2-7; Lk 5:18-25; 7:47-49; Mk 2:3-12.

161. Cf Jn 3:17.

162. Jn 20:22; Mt 18:18; cf also, as regards Peter, Mt 16:19. Blessed Isaac of Stella in one of his talks emphasizes the full communion of Christ with the church in the forgiveness of sins: "The church can forgive nothing without Christ and Christ does not wish to forgive anything without the church. The church can forgive nothing except to a penitent, that is to say, to a person whom Christ has touched with his grace: Christ does not wish to consider anything forgiven in a person who despises the church": *Sermo 11 (In Dominica II Post Epiphaniam, I): PL* 194, 1729.

163. Cf Mt 12:49f; Mk 3:33f; Lk 8:20f; Rom 8:29: "the firstborn among many brethren."

164. Cf Heb 2:17; 4:15.

165. Cf Mt 18:12f; Lk 15:4-6.

166. Cf Lk 5:31f.

167. Cf Mt 22:16.

168. Cf Acts 10:42.

169. Cf Jn 8:16.

170. Cf the address to the penitentiaries of the Roman patriarchal basilicas and to the priest confessors at the closing of the Jubilee of the Redemption (July 9, 1984): *L'Osservatore Romano,* July 9-10, 1984.

171. Jn 8:11.

172. Cf Ti 3:4.

173. Cf Council of Trent, Session XIV *De Sacramento Poenitentiae,* Chap. 1 and Canon 1: *Conciliorum Oecumenicorum Decreta,* 703f, 711 (DS 1668-1670, 1701).

174. *Lumen Gentium,* 11.

175. Cf Council of Trent, Session XIV, *De Sacramento Poenitentiae*, Chap. 1 and Canon 1: *Conciliorum Oecumenicorum Decreta*, ed. cit., 703f, 711 (DS 1668-1670, 1701).

176. Cf Constitution on the Sacred Liturgy *Sacrosanctum Concilium*, 72.

177. Cf *Rituale Romanum ex Decreto Sacrosancti Concilii Oecumenici Vaticani II Instauratum, Auctoritate Pauli VI Promulgatum: Ordo Paenitentiae*, Vatican Polyglot Press, 1974.

178. The Council of Trent uses the attenuated expression *"ad instar actus iudicialis"* (Session XIV *De Sacramento Poenitentiae*, Chap. 6: *Conciliorum Oecumenicorum Decreta*, ed. cit., 707 (DS 1685), in order to emphasize the difference from human tribunals. The new Rite of Penance makes reference to this function, Nos. 6b and 10a.

179. Cf Lk 5:31f: "Those who are well have no need of a physician, but those who are sick" concluding: "I have...come to call...sinners to repentance"; Lk 9:2: "And he sent them out to preach the kingdom of God and to heal." The image of Christ the physician takes on new and striking elements if we compare it with the figure of the Servant of Yahweh, of whom the Book of Isaiah prophesies that "he has borne our griefs and carried our sorrows" and that with his stripes we are healed" (Is 53:4f).

180. St. Augustine, *Sermo* 82, 8: *PL* 38, 511.

181. Ibid., *Sermo*, 352, 3, 8:9: *PL* 39, 1558f.

182. Cf *Ordo Paenitentiae*, 6c.

183. Even the pagans recognized the existence of "divine" moral laws which have "always" existed and which are written in the depths of the human heart, cf Sophocles *(Antigone*, vv. 450-460) and Aristotle *(Rhetor.*, Book I, Chap. 15, 1375 a-b).

184. On the role of conscience cf what I said at the general audience of March 14, 1984, 3: *Insegnamenti, VII*, 1 (1984), 683.

185. Cf Council of Trent, Session XIV *De Sacramento Poenitentiae*, Chap. 4, *De Contritione: Conciliorum Oecumenicorum Decreta*, ed. cit., 705 (DS 1676-1677). Of course, in order to approach the sacrament of penance it is sufficient to have attrition, or imperfect repentance, due more to fear than to love. But in the sphere of the sacrament, the penitent, under the action of the grace that he receives, *"ex attrito fit contritus,"* since penance really operates in the person who is well-disposed to conversion in love: cf Council of Trent, ibid., ed. cit., 705 (DS 1678).

186. *Ordo Paenitentiae*, 6c.

187. Cf Ps 51(50):12.

188. I had occasion to speak of these fundamental aspects of penance at the general audiences of May 19, 1982: *Insegnamenti* V, 2 (1982), 1758ff; February 28, 1979: *Insegnamenti* II (1979), 475-478; March 21, 1984: *Insegnamenti VII*, 1 (1984), 720-722. See also the norms of the Code of Canon Law concerning the place for administering the sacrament and concerning confessionals (Canon 964, 2-3).

189. I dealt with this subject concisely at the general audience of March 7,

1984: *Insegnamenti* VII, 1 (1984), 631-633.

  190. Cf Gn 4:7, 15.

  191. Cf 2 Sm 12.

  192. Cf Lk 15:17-21.

  193. Cf *Presbyterorum Ordinis*, 18.

  194. *Ordo Paenitentiae*, 7b.

  195. Cf ibid., 17.

  196. Canons 961-963.

  197. Cf Ez 18:23.

  198. Cf Is 42:3; Mt 12:20.

  199. Cf *Familiaris Consortio*, 84: *AAS* 74 (1982), 184-186.

  200. Cf 1 Pt 1:1f; 3:8.

  201. Ibid., 3:9, 13.

  202. Ibid., 3:8, 9, 13.

  203. Ibid., 3:17.

  204. Litany of the Sacred Heart, cf 1 Jn 2:2; Eph 2:14; Rom 3:25; 5:11.

  205. Pope John Paul II, General Audience Address of December 7, 1983, No. 2: *Insegnamenti*, VI, 2 (1983), 1264.

  206. Ibid., General Audience Address of January 4, 1984: *Insegnamenti*, VII, 1 (1984), 16-18.

  207. Cf Rom 1:5; 16:26.

BOOKS & MEDIA

The Daughters of St. Paul operate book and media centers at the following addresses. Visit, call or write the one nearest you today, or find us on the World Wide Web, www.pauline.org

CALIFORNIA

3908 Sepulveda Blvd, Culver City, CA 90230   310-397-8676

5945 Balboa Avenue, San Diego, CA 92111   858-565-9181

46 Geary Street, San Francisco, CA 94108   415-781-5180

FLORIDA

145 S.W. 107th Avenue, Miami, FL 33174   305-559-6715

HAWAII

1143 Bishop Street, Honolulu, HI 96813   808-521-2731

Neighbor Islands call: 800-259-8463

ILLINOIS

172 North Michigan Avenue, Chicago, IL 60601   312-346-4228

LOUISIANA

4403 Veterans Memorial Blvd, Metairie, LA 70006   504-887-7631

MASSACHUSETTS

885 Providence Hwy, Dedham, MA 02026   781-326-5385

MISSOURI

9804 Watson Road, St. Louis, MO 63126   314-965-3512

NEW JERSEY

561 U.S. Route 1, Wick Plaza, Edison, NJ 08817   732-572-1200

NEW YORK

150 East 52nd Street, New York, NY 10022   212-754-1110

78 Fort Place, Staten Island, NY 10301   718-447-5071

PENNSYLVANIA

9171-A Roosevelt Blvd, Philadelphia, PA 19114   215-676-9494

SOUTH CAROLINA

243 King Street, Charleston, SC 29401   843-577-0175

TENNESSEE

4811 Poplar Avenue, Memphis, TN 38117   901-761-2987

TEXAS

114 Main Plaza, San Antonio, TX 78205   210-224-8101

VIRGINIA

1025 King Street, Alexandria, VA 22314   703-549-3806

CANADA

3022 Dufferin Street, Toronto, ON M6B 3T5   416-781-9131

1155 Yonge Street, Toronto, ON M4T 1W2   416-934-3440

¡También somos su fuente para libros, videos y música en español!